WITHDRAWN

Past Masters
General Editor Keith Thomas

Tolstoy

Past Masters

AQUINAS Anthony Kenny
ARISTOTLE Jonathan Barnes
BACH Denis Arnold
FRANCIS BACON Anthony
 Quinton
BAYLE Elisabeth Labrousse
BERKELEY J. O. Urmson
THE BUDDHA Michael Carrithers
BURKE C. B. Macpherson
CARLYLE A. L. Le Quesne
CHAUCER George Kane
CLAUSEWITZ Michael Howard
COBBETT Raymond Williams
COLERIDGE Richard Holmes
CONFUCIUS Raymond Dawson
DANTE George Holmes
DARWIN Jonathan Howard
DIDEROT Peter France
GEORGE ELIOT Rosemary Ashton
ENGELS Terrell Carver
GALILEO Stillman Drake
GOETHE T. J. Reed

HEGEL Peter Singer
HOMER Jasper Griffin
HUME A. J. Ayer
JESUS Humphrey Carpenter
KANT Roger Scruton
LAMARCK L. J. Jordanova
LEIBNIZ G. MacDonald Ross
LOCKE John Dunn
MACHIAVELLI Quentin Skinner
MARX Peter Singer
MENDEL Vitezslav Orel
MONTAIGNE Peter Burke
THOMAS MORE Anthony Kenny
WILLIAM MORRIS Peter Stansky
MUHAMMAD Michael Cook
NEWMAN Owen Chadwick
PASCAL Alban Krailsheimer
PETRARCH Nicholas Mann
PLATO R. M. Hare
PROUST Derwent May
TOLSTOY Henry Gifford

Forthcoming

AUGUSTINE Henry Chadwick
BAGEHOT Colin Matthew
BERGSON Leszek Kolakowski
JOSEPH BUTLER R. G. Frey
CERVANTES P. E. Russell
COPERNICUS Owen Gingerich
DESCARTES Tom Sorell
DISRAELI John Vincent
ERASMUS John McConica
GIBBON J. W. Burrow
GODWIN Alan Ryan
HERZEN Aileen Kelly
JEFFERSON Jack P. Greene
JOHNSON Pat Rogers
KIERKEGAARD Patrick Gardiner
LEONARDO E. H. Gombrich

LINNAEUS W. T. Stearn
MILL William Thomas
MONTESQUIEU Judith Shklar
NEWTON P. M. Rattansi
ROUSSEAU Robert Wokler
RUSKIN George P. Landow
RUSSELL John G. Slater
SHAKESPEARE Germaine Greer
ADAM SMITH D. D. Raphael
SOCRATES Bernard Williams
SPINOZA Roger Scruton
VICO Peter Burke
VIRGIL Jasper Griffin
WYCLIF Anthony Kenny

and others

Henry Gifford

TOLSTOY

Oxford   New York

OXFORD UNIVERSITY PRESS

Oxford University Press, Walton Street, Oxford OX2 6DP

London New York Toronto
Delhi Bombay Calcutta Madras Karachi
Kuala Lumpur Singapore Hong Kong Tokyo
Nairobi Dar es Salaam Cape Town
Melbourne Auckland

and associated companies in
Beirut Berlin Ibadan Mexico City Nicosia

© Henry Gifford 1982

First published 1982 as an Oxford University Press paperback
and simultaneously in a hardback edition
Hardback reprinted with corrections 1983, 1985

British Library Cataloguing in Publication Data
Gifford, Henry
Tolstoy. − (Past masters)
1. Tolstoy, Leo, Count − Biography
I. Title II. Series
8891.7'3'3 PG3385
ISBN 0-19-287545-0
ISBN 0-19-287544-2 Pbk

Set by Datamove Ltd.
Printed in Great Britain
at the University Press, Oxford
by Eric Buckley
Printer to the University

Preface

A book on Tolstoy in this series will necessarily be concerned with his thought. In later life he became widely known as a thinker, a religious leader and critic of modern civilisation. But primarily he counts as an artist, and it was the novels and stories that won him an audience for his ideas. Two chapters are given to the major novels, *War and Peace* and *Anna Karenina*. Other fictional writings are discussed in chapters about particular aspects of his life and thought. Tolstoy's views on education, on religion, on personal conduct and social action, and on art are important enough to be treated in separate chapters. At the beginning I describe briefly his relation to his own time and country, and the difficulties he met in establishing his vocation. Finally I attempt to weigh Tolstoy's significance for the present time.

Commentaries on Tolstoy are legion, and many of them distinguished. My debts to earlier criticism are too numerous to mention, although certain works are cited in the Bibliographical Note. Anyone familiar with the subject will be aware how much I owe to the magisterial studies of Boris Eykhenbaum, and also to the work of the most candid and judicious interpreter among Tolstoy's contemporaries, his English biographer, Aylmer Maude.

I am very grateful to Virginia Llewellyn Smith for much helpful comment on the text, and to Margaret Milsom for typing the manuscript.

Bristol
March 1981   HENRY GIFFORD

Abbreviations

The following abbreviations are used for reference:

A   *What is Art? and Essays on Art by Tolstóy*, translated by Aylmer Maude (Oxford, 1930; reprint of 1950)

L   *Tolstoy's Letters*, vol. I 1828—1879; vol. II, 1880–1910 selected, edited and translated by R. F. Christian (London, 1978)

M   Aylmer Maude, *The Life of Tolstóy*, 2 vols. (Oxford, 1930)

G   *Leo Tolstoy: A Critical Anthology*, edited by Henry Gifford (London, 1971)

References to passages in the novels specify book (when relevant), part and chapter. Thus, for *War and Peace* iv ii 12 signifies the twelfth chapter of the second part of Book Four. *Anna Karenina* and *Resurrection* are divided into parts: II vii signifies the seventh chapter in the second part.

Contents

1 The position of Tolstoy

Leo Nikolayevich Tolstoy was troubled to an exceptional degree by the anxiety to define always where he stood. His whole life was devoted to seeking and explaining his position. It is no frivolous comment that from the beginning Tolstoy's problem was Tolstoy. The centre of all his enquiries lay in himself, and to the very last he was still trying to make his position unassailable not so much from the criticism of others as from his own doubts.

Tolstoy left home in 1851, accompanying his soldier brother Nikolay to the Caucasus, and soon joining the army as a cadet. He set out a dissatisfied and restless young nobleman: his spiritual journey was to end some sixty years later in flight from his family. It proved to be long and arduous, full of checks and digressions, but sustained by a single purpose. To follow him is to cut a path through the controversies that beset Russia in the years leading up to violent revolution and seemingly irreversible change. Tolstoy, the great dissident, never failed to find himself guided by instinct to the problem of the hour. It is impossible to engage fully with his thought unless one recognises its significance for the Russia in which he lived. Tolstoy may well be the Russian writer who appears least inaccessible to readers in the West. He is genuinely a participant in that world literature foreseen by Goethe. *War and Peace* is profoundly Russian in its sentiments, but not the more alien for that to our understanding. *Anna Karenina* seems as near to us as the greatest novels in the English language – even more completely ours than an American novel such as *Moby Dick*. Yet Tolstoy's concerns were specifically Russian concerns, pressing in his own time. Tolstoy's response cannot be altogether rightly appreciated if we ignore the traditions in which he wrote and the circumstances of his life.

No single writer, even the greatest, embodies the whole experience of the age. But when this has been granted we may contend that Tolstoy's life can be seen as expressing with a rare amplitude the aspirations and perplexities of Russia in its gathering crisis. The ninety volumes of his collected works in the admirable Moscow edition (1928–58) form a testimony to his time, the record of how it must have felt to be alive in that particular country facing deep and perhaps intractable problems. Through the life of Tolstoy we can bring to a focus the life of his people, which later events have made a matter of interest to the whole world.

The fourth and youngest son of Count Nikolay Tolstoy, he lived from 1828 until 1910. In political terms (which are always important for the understanding of Russian literature) this means that he grew to manhood just at the time when a new force was beginning to work a significant change in the self-awareness of his countrymen. Tolstoy came of age the year after Vissarion Belinsky died. Belinsky was the leading critic of his generation, and an ardent democrat. To him in the 1840s more than to any of his associates it had fallen to mobilise this new force – the Russian intelligentsia. Missionaries of the idea (in a country where political opposition had mainly to express itself through ideas alone, in open or veiled form), high-minded, earnest and intolerant, the more radical followers of Belinsky in the next decade would move towards eventual control of the leading literary journal, the *Contemporary*, in which Tolstoy's own earliest writings were published. The crucial debate of the 1840s about national destiny between Slavophils and Westerners was to rage and involve Tolstoy himself for many years. It is reflected in his two major works of the 1860s and 1870s, *War and Peace* and *Anna Karenina*.

By that time the most effective leaders of the intelligentsia were populist thinkers of the utilitarian school, Westerners rather than Slavophils, committed to democratic ideals and to the progress of science, and at odds with their predecessors in the Western camp, enlightened members of the nobility. The man who could claim to have replaced Belinsky as the mentor of thinking young Russians, N. G. Chernyshevsky, was born in the same year as Tolstoy. He and his younger associate, N. A. Dobrolyubov, were plebeians in origin, the sons of priests, and themselves former seminarists. It was the so-called *raznochintsy* or 'men of various rank', children of the clergy, of merchants, or minor officials, who came to dominate the intelligentsia. At the same time the landed nobility, once their serfs had been emancipated in 1861, began to make way for a new class of entrepreneurs and financiers.

Tolstoy, who as a young man was highly conscious of his rank, belonged to a titled family which was large and had some distinguished members. He could not be expected to welcome the change of outlook in his generation. The intelligentsia was alien to him because those who belonged to it, like Molotov the hero of N. G. Pomyalovsky's novel *Plebeian Happiness* (1860), had no ties with the soil. Molotov's childhood never knew the shelter of ancestral limetrees, and this 'meant a great deal to him'. Their absence gave Molotov the ideal freedom of the plebeian (*raznochinets*) – his origins being so obscure that, un-like a merchant's son or a seminarist, or a displaced nobleman, he had no established order from which to break away. This made him paradoxically the most fortunate of 'new men', the one who came into the intelligentsia with the soundest of all credentials.

But Tolstoy was born to the possession of limetrees. He in-herited from his mother's family the estate of Yasnaya Polyana in central Russia, where he had spent much of his childhood, being brought up, after the early deaths of his mother and father, under the guardianship of two aunts. Throughout life, and especially from the late 1850s when he settled there, Yas-naya Polyana was inseparable from his being. This made even more poignant his final desertion of the place, followed so soon by his death at a small railway station on the steppes. Yasnaya Polyana was for Tolstoy a way of life, a support to him and at times a refuge, the focus of ancient pieties, and his window upon Russia. When Levin, the surrogate for Tolstoy himself in *Anna Karenina*, has been refused by the girl he wants to marry, he recovers confidence the moment he has returned to his native place. The 'large old-fashioned house' was 'a whole world to Levin. It was the world in which his father and mother had lived and died. They had lived a life which appeared to him ideally perfect, and which he had dreamed of renewing with a wife and family of his own' (I xxvii).

A dozen or more years before writing those lines Tolstoy had confessed (in a fragment of 1858, called 'Summer in the Country'): 'Without my Yasnaya Polyana I find it difficult to imagine Russia and my attitude towards her. Without Yasnaya Polyana I shall perhaps see more clearly the general laws needed for my country, but I shall not love it so passionately.' At this time Tolstoy, like his neighbours, was considering what effect emancipating the serfs would have upon the class to which he belonged, 'small landowners who have lived in the country, were born in the country, and love their own corner.' But when emancipation came in 1861 Tolstoy did not have to give up Yasnaya Polyana. It was there at the very end of the 1850s that he had opened a village school, teaching in it himself and publishing a journal to record the experiment and to promote his ideas. This he named revealingly *Yasnaya Polyana*.

The possession of this estate enabled Tolstoy to write for himself. He could publish in his own time (except when temporarily short of money), and did not have to depend upon editors and publishers, or, like Pushkin eventually, upon the favour and even financial help of the Tsar. He was not the only Russian writer of his day with that advantage. Ivan Turgenev, for example, owned a very much larger property in the same region. But Turgenev was content for the latter part of his life to settle abroad, drawing revenues from his estate and visiting it, if at all, in the summer months. Tolstoy resembles their common friend the poet Afanasy Fet, who also worked his land, with a shrewdness and tenacity indeed that Tolstoy could not equal. Levin in the novel is unlike his associates because he takes no interest in activities that lie outside the landowner's daily round, and existence without the estate to manage would retain no meaning for him.

Tolstoy certainly agreed with Levin in his belief about the foundations of human life. He had no liking for urban civilisation, fast becoming industrial in the West, and even in Russia beginning to go the same way. He cherished the rural simplicities which had governed the lives of his fathers. Their idyll had been marred by an institution he knew to be unjust, serfdom, and he welcomed its end. But the patriarchal order in the country satisfied his emotions and seemed to him morally right.

The basis of Tolstoy's thinking was always to remain agrarian, in a way not common among writers of this persuasion more or less contemporary with him. Two such in English nineteenth-century literature, Wordsworth and Hardy, are onlookers in the regions they made peculiarly their own. For them the act of possession was purely imaginative: they were writers with no rival occupation, though one had been an architect and the other held a sinecure. Tolstoy, the most celebrated writer of his age, never became one in the exclusive sense.

Yasnaya Polyana, then, its traditions, routine and security, gave him a firm footing of his own. He acquired first-hand knowledge of the peasant in the field, just as in the army he had known him as a private soldier. The populist critic N. K. Mikhaylovsky complained that he overlooked or distorted certain attitudes of the peasants, exaggerating for example their naïveté and proneness to superstition; but what Lenin once said to Gorky is still near the truth: 'Before this count there was no genuine peasant in Russian literature.'

Despite a few unsatisfactory years (1844–7) spent at the University of Kazan, where he changed from oriental languages to law without completing the course, Tolstoy's education was almost entirely self-directed. In contrast with Turgenev and others who had studied Hegel in Berlin he is the backwoodsman, even the primitive. His reading was tireless, intense and unmethodical. It answered his needs of the moment, and his fiercely sceptical mind always preferred to work out solutions from scratch. He prided himself on making his own discoveries, reconstituting for example the theories of the Physiocrats who preceded Adam Smith and held that agricultural labour alone is productive. Turgenev was very impatient when this 'autodidact . . . took it upon himself to philosophise', and sometimes had reason to be.

Yet Tolstoy was a formidable though uneven thinker, often rightly contemptuous of abstraction and shallowness in his contemporaries. The radicals who took Belinsky's place turned from the Hegelianism of his day to Bentham, Mill, Spencer and Comte. Thus the ideas encountered by George Eliot as a young woman soon afterwards formed the outlook of Chernyshevsky and Dobrolyubov. But Tolstoy's cast of thought had been determined by the previous century. He grew up on the pattern rather of a critically minded aristocrat in Catherine's reign, with that liking for common sense and confidence in the judgement of the intelligent layman which is characteristic of the Enlightenment. The reductive energies of his mind are Voltairean, and so too is his intolerance of mystery. Rousseau's combination of powerful sentiment with lucid exposition became very much Tolstoy's own. Like most thinkers in the main eighteenth-century stream, he clung to the notion of a world stable in its system, with fixed moral foundations, and he wanted to believe in the absolute freedom of the individual. Tolstoy rejected passionately the historicism that separated his own time from the age in which he felt at home. He shared no hopes for political change in Russia on the way to a millennium. His sole preoccupation was the cleansing of conscience, the pursuit not of general happiness but of personal rectitude, the recovery of right feeling and uncorrupted judgement. He often seemed a traditionalist at bay.

Yet he was no traditionalist in the mould of Burke, though proud like him to 'bear the stamp of our forefathers' and cherishing the prejudices that seemed in accord with nature. The atmosphere of his mind is much closer to that of the unromantic Swift. He became progressively more caustic about the present than elegiac of the past. Tolstoy's beliefs were only valuable to him for their resistance to his immense critical powers. The destructive force of his mind has led to comparisons with Nietzsche. Tolstoy's thinking is a protest against the course of modern society. But his sense of things – the bedrock of conviction that no logic could undermine – was reactionary. It had not the ultimate recklessness of Nietzsche.

His most productive years followed the Emancipation of the serfs in 1861, when the process of economic change started to accelerate in Russia. By 1908, the year of his eightieth birthday, he stood alone, the monument to a past age, having survived by a quarter of a century the great novelists who had been his contemporaries, Turgenev, Goncharov, Dostoyevsky. He had lived on to become the friend of Chekhov, and to eye with uneasy interest Maxim Gorky who would one day promulgate the doctrine of 'socialist realism'. In his fiction and latterly more often in tracts and parables for the masses, Tolstoy had elaborated a teaching not accepted in full by many (though it counted Gandhi among its adherents). Yet he had gained an immense moral authority. His mere presence seemed to reprove the greed and injustice of Russian society on the brink of catastrophic change.

Turgenev in 1883 at the point of death had implored Tolstoy to give up his new role as preacher and return to literature. But by that time Tolstoy had repudiated *War and Peace* and *Anna Karenina* as morally repugnant to him. For the last thirty years of his life he struggled to renounce all he had been, with no more backsliding, and to emulate the piety and submission of the simple. It was an unequal contest, and Tolstoy to the last remained Tolstoy, though in bonds.

He was inescapably a writer, whatever Turgenev may have feared. The Tolstoy who most accurately and subtly defines his position is the novelist in whose work the manifold nature of consciousness can be revealed. The novelist, like the poet, deals not with concepts but with the experience out of which concepts arise. Tolstoy's ideas when formulated – and he was adept at doing this – are more restricted in meaning. A novel that has been lived through intensely by its author does not demonstrate an argument. It tries rather to record the sense of situations and to discern the links between them. And this is what the critic must undertake in evaluating Tolstoy's work.

2 Testing his vocation

To judge from Tolstoy's first fictional narrative, *Childhood* (1852), which he wrote while still serving in the Caucasus, the habit of introspection began with him very early. Nikolenka in that story displays an astonishing power of self-analysis. No child was ever more intent upon interpreting his own motives, or so morbidly suspicious of vanity in himself and others. He lives fully in his senses, like all children. Nothing is lost upon him – every detail, for instance, of the scene when on a bright day he goes hunting, the humming of insects motionless in the air, the smell of wormwood, straw and horse sweat, the white cobwebs floating or laid on the stubble. Most of all he attends to the expression of faces, the unconscious gestures that betray feeling, the deeper significance behind spoken words. Nikolenka is an uncomfortable observer of human weakness, with a child's appalling honesty. Even·when very young, he looks on life, and on himself participating in it, as an artist does. His perceptions are candid and penetrating, with a deeper self-knowledge than that of the adults. At his mother's funeral, Nikolenka is shocked at not being able to feel a more compelling grief, and critical of his father for playing the part of principal mourner too well. He can distinguish between the worked-up hysteria of his grandmother, and the genuine sorrow of an old servant who can yet give her mind to rationing out the sugar.

From 1847, when still a student, Tolstoy kept a diary. It was here he developed the alert self-scrutiny which gave him such a formidable insight into human nature. With a few interruptions the diaries continued until he finally left home in October 1910. Boris Eykhenbaum, outstanding among Tolstoy scholars, has shown how important these were for the development of his art, which began in their pages. They monitored his progress severely. Much of what he saw in the mirror offended him as being ugly and shameful.

Too often in the earliest years he is found following in a humourless way the example of Benjamin Franklin. All through life he was addicted to making rules and somewhat pedantically framing classifications. He becomes his own schoolmaster, fertile in precept and usually displeased. Tolstoy's youthful depravity was nothing uncommon, his breaches of honour or trust not remarkable. He gambled as others did, having to sell off part of his wooden manor house to clear the debt; he was fairly promiscuous; he could be overbearing and quarrelsome. But he took a savage pleasure in exaggerating his deficiencies. At the beginning of the Crimean war, not long before he secured a posting to besieged Sevastopol, he looked hard at himself and drew up a report. It was almost wholly unflattering. He saw a man ill-favoured, awkward, uneducated; arrogant but shy; vain, idle, inconsistent; and with the ambition of glory.

Sometimes he envisages a grandiose task – to write the first true history of contemporary Europe; to edit a highly improving journal; to devise a plan for reforming the army, or rules for managing his estate. In Sevastopol comes a 'tremendous thought': he must found a new religion, rational Christianity stripped of mystery and dogma, so that bliss may be attained on earth. Doubtful of his will, only too conscious of how little he has yet done, Tolstoy believes himself to be designated for great ends. In spite of everything he is convinced of his moral superiority to other men.

But this moody castigator of his sins was interested not only in character improvement and the benefit of mankind. He had been fascinated by the self-revelations of Rousseau and Sterne. Everywhere in those first diaries there is evidence of literary talent pressing for an outlet. He was genuinely concerned with his moral condition; he wanted badly to find something durable he could believe in. At the same time the act of recording his observations delighted him for its own sake. The diaries are also a writer's workshop, littered with sketches, notes and projects. Eykhenbaum maintains he was essentially more absorbed in the mastery of a method than in the mastery of his own nature. Just before starting on *Childhood* he had taken a first step from his diary into fiction, *The Story of Yesterday*. Already, Eykhenbaum points out, the method of analysis has given him the device called by the formalist critic Viktor Shklovsky 'making it strange' (*ostraneniye*), when he stands outside himself to watch the absent-minded movements of his own body. The anxiety for moral betterment was real; but the keenest satisfaction came from his newly found art. It would remain always a problem to reconcile the demands of art with those of living.

For subjects he turned to his own past (with some imaginative extensions) in *Childhood* and its less noteworthy sequels, *Boyhood* (1854) and *Youth* (1857). He wrote too of army life in the Caucasus – a raid or a wood-felling expedition into hostile territory. He described in *A Landowner's Morning* (1856) the sheer disbelief with which the peasants listened to any proposals for land reform made by their master. Tolstoy is a writer to whom Belinsky's words about Turgenev also apply: 'He must always keep to the ground of actuality.' It unsettled him to be separated from his own immediate interests (as we shall find when he was writing *Anna Karenina*). The actuality he encountered in his apprentice years as a writer was very rewarding for Tolstoy. This was particularly so when he served as an artillery officer in the Crimean war. His three famous despatches, *Sevastopol in December*, *Sevastopol in May*, and *Sevastopol in August 1855*, rendered the truth of war so arrestingly that all educated Russians from the Tsar to remote provincials shared the experience. Literary fame had been granted him in the shortest possible time.

Misgivings about his capacity as a writer had been very acute not long before he submitted *Childhood* to Nikolay Nekrasov, editor of the *Contemporary*. What talent had he in comparison with the newly established men? 'Decidedly none at all,' he thought. So Nekrasov's favourable reply made him 'happy to the point of idiocy'. After the success of the first two Sevastopol sketches he resolved that the only career for him must be literature – 'to write and write'. By November 1855 he was in Petersburg, already a civilian in all but name, and an author among authors.

Turgenev, foremost among Russian writers of fiction at this time, had taken an interest in him from the beginning. He wrote the very day before Tolstoy made his resolution, imploring him to leave the front and its dangers. 'For your own sake, and for Literature,' he insisted, 'come!' Tolstoy's problem in the next few years would be whether to accord literature the capital letter Turgenev so reverently gave it.

On arriving in Petersburg he had every reason to feel confident. Tolstoy was welcomed as the most promising recruit to the best journal in Russia. Chernyshevsky, whose influence was becoming powerful, wrote two articles about him that were decisive. A rather dull critic usually, here he shone. Tolstoy, he proclaimed, had a marvellous insight into 'the dialectic of the soul', surpassing even the cool precision of Lermontov in his prose tale *A Hero of Our Time* (1841). Further he noted an immediacy and purity of feeling, which brought to mind Shakespeare's heroines. It is not an absurd comparison. Tolstoy does resemble them in his natural candour and a kind of innocence. Chernyshevsky predicted that psychological finesse and a sure moral instinct would never desert him.

Turgenev foretold a great future for Tolstoy, who had once been in despair of emulating his *Sketches of a Sportsman* (1847–51). 'When this young wine has fermented', he wrote, 'it will make a beverage fit for the gods.' The fermentation was very troublesome. Tolstoy soon began to alienate Petersburg literary men by his contrariness. He spoke as a Slavophil among Westerners, a Westerner among Slavophils. His deep-seated impulse to recusancy made him nowhere at home. Turgenev, Nekrasov and Chernyshevsky were all anxious to save Tolstoy from himself. This wayward but astonishing talent must not be allowed to fail Russian literature.

That Tolstoy was no less dissatisfied with himself is clear. And it would be wrong to put everything down to his cross-grained temperament. He did at this time often behave badly, assuming the role of an ill-bred aristocrat or a soldier contemptuous of civilians. But his disagreements with almost everybody had their source in more than spleen or bigotry. He knew there was little common ground between himself and the others.

His relations with Turgenev could scarcely have been expected to stay harmonious. Turgenev, a very civilised man, the consummate Westerner, was shocked by Tolstoy's brutal rejection of all that the liberals honoured. Tolstoy on his side suspected Turgenev of frivolity and coldness. It would amaze him when reading *On the Eve* in 1860 that Turgenev with so fine a sensibility could slip without knowing it into the banal. Nor was Tolstoy willing to become a professional author on the pattern set for him by Turgenev. His project of schooling Tolstoy when their assumptions were so very different had no chance of success. Turgenev's bantering posture of a senior coaxing along his junior was unfortunate, and his unsureness of touch surprising in one usually so tactful. It must have jarred on Tolstoy to hear from Paris that *Childhood* and *Youth* had created a 'furore' among Russian ladies there, so that he was in mode 'more than the crinoline'. Turgenev could never accept that Tolstoy's seeming perversities were inseparable from the strength of his talent. He longed for Tolstoy to enlarge his horizon, and warned him against system-making. 'System is only the tail of truth,' he explained, 'but truth is like a lizard; it will leave its tail in your hand – and run away.' But Tolstoy could not have been Tolstoy without the passion for system, however strongly his scepticism bore down on it. Turgenev continued to grieve over the misdirection, as he saw it, of prodigious creative powers.

All through 1859 the aristocrats in the *Contemporary* group were under attack from Dobrolyubov on account of their reformist attitudes and their appreciation of art as an end in itself. An essay of Dobrolyubov's using *On the Eve* to support his own revolutionary views finally drove Turgenev to break with the journal. In the conflict between the 'aesthetes', as their opponents called them, and the radicals, or 'literary Robespierres' in Turgenev's accusing phrase, Tolstoy's sympathies for a time lay with the former. In 1858 he even proposed setting up a journal with Turgenev and others among the 'aesthetes' to save literature from the 'sordid stream of politics' which was sweeping into it (L 116). Now that the idea of Emancipation was being mooted by government, political issues took on a new sharpness. The fragile consensus between liberals and revolutionary democrats fell apart. Nekrasov, though sharing the class background of the 'aesthetes', went across to the new men, the 'seminarists' disliked by Turgenev.

The term 'aesthete' may suggest to the Western reader the equivalent of Mallarmé or Pater. That would be very misleading in the case of Turgenev who, while deploring Dobrolyubov's starkly ideological bias, could not help feeling some admiration for revolutionary commitment. All Russian writers in that age had to reckon with the views of Belinsky; and Belinsky had taught them that their function was to bring society to self-awareness by defining the new 'types' thrown up by 'history'. On this Turgenev agreed with the radicals. What they objected to in the 'aesthetes' was a concern with the amenities rather than the transformation of life. He could not share their belief that Nikolay Gogol, supreme in comic fantasy but taken by them, as by Belinsky, to be simply an outright critic of social abuses, was more necessary to know than Pushkin, whose instinctive harmony seemed hopelessly out of touch with their own time and its discords.

Tolstoy was no natural ally for the 'aesthetes', considerations of class loyalty apart. However, he soon picked his quarrel with the opposing camp. He detested the convictions of the intelligentsia. Nekrasov wrote in alarm to Turgenev about the hostility Tolstoy was showing to 'that tendency which until now he had been serving himself and which every honourable man in Russia serves'. Where, he asked, could you find another 'living and honourable' tendency 'except in exposure and protest'? But Tolstoy had told him people were deceived who thought it 'very nice to be *angry*, *irritable* and *malicious*' (L 60; Tolstoy's italics). Something of patrician pride came into his dislike of the radicals. He mocked at their jargon afterwards in his comedy *An Infected Family* (1863). However, more than social distaste was involved. Tolstoy was at odds with progressive opinion of all shades because he challenged the dogma of historical advance.

Already by the end of 1857 Turgenev was becoming disturbed by his intransigence. Tolstoy had told him it was not enough to be a mere man of letters, and in reply he asked, What, then, was Tolstoy – 'an officer? a landowner? a philosopher? the founder of a new religious doctrine? an official? a man on the make?' Exasperation led him to scatter his shots too wide, but some of them struck home. Tolstoy's fiction at the end of the 1850s was judged to be failing. His novel *Family*

Happiness (1859) on the maturing of married love between a girl and a much older man, and two stories, *Lucerne* (1857) and *Albert* (1858) – each a heavy-handed defence of art, arising from Tolstoy's temporary support of the 'aesthetes' – aroused little interest. He had still to complete a story from this period which, when it came out in 1863, delighted Turgenev – *The Cossacks*. So far as concerned literature Tolstoy was gravely disheartened. He had broken with his last allies, the 'aesthetes'; attention of the public to his work seemed to have melted away; he no longer counted in the world of letters. Turgenev had been right to think he was in search of a new role.

There ensued an interval of some years during which he claimed to have given up authorship. From this time for the whole half-century of life remaining to him Tolstoy's dedication to literature would be shaken by crises of doubt. The impulse to write was immensely strong, and he was to produce thousands upon thousands of pages: novels, stories, plays, and then a gathering flood of treatises on moral, religious, social and educational matters, programmes of action, tracts for the times. But he stood, as it were, outside literature, no longer one of the fraternity; still keenly interested in what others were doing, but aloof from their purposes and unfriendly towards their conception of literature. It would be absurd not to call him a professional. He never affected to disdain the writer's calling as unworthy of an aristocrat. But he chafed at the limitations of a single-minded concern with literature such as Turgenev's. For him to become a professional author in that sense was impossible.

Tolstoy always had powerful incentives to be doing. If in his dispassionate analysis he gave the impression of being detached, it was the better to understand some problem demanding action. When halted in his literary work, as at the end of the 1850s, he would turn for relief to a practical task. In February 1860 he wrote to Fet that literature as practised by Turgenev and the playwright A.N. Ostrovsky was not enough. An urgent duty confronted him to help the peasants and 'teach Marfa and Taras at least a little of what we know' (L 137).

3 Lessons of the village school

Tolstoy had begun to occupy himself with teaching peasant children from his own village in the autumn of 1859. He did this for three years, also travelling abroad to study educational methods, and serving in 1861–2 as Arbiter of the Peace, an officer specially appointed to negotiate land settlements between landlords and peasants after the Emancipation of the serfs.

As a young man he had read Rousseau on education. The influence upon him at that time of *Émile* was, he admitted later, 'enormous', and it endured. The didactic impulse in Tolstoy was now given free play; he claimed to have found teaching these children 'as natural ... as breathing the air'. More was involved than the hope of a new (and less uneasy) vocation. Olenin, the young aristocrat from the capital, had gone to the Cossacks in Tolstoy's story of that name so as to become a child of nature. Tolstoy himself now appeared to have undone the effects of his upbringing as Olenin never could. Unlike the narrator of Turgenev's story *Bezhin Meadow* (1851), who is privileged to overhear a group of herd-boys one summer night, but comes no closer to them, Tolstoy in his school was almost an elder brother among the children.

Characteristically he sought the answer to a much-canvassed problem on his own doorstep. He kept his eyes on the small peasant boy whose life would be spent in the fields, whose needs were practical, and whose instincts must be cherished. The primitive force and restrictedness of Tolstoy's views on education contrast strangely with those of his contemporary Newman in *The Idea of a University* (1859). Newman's object was to train 'the true citizen and gentleman', and to do this he relied on the university. But Tolstoy felt the same contempt for professors as for doctors and military experts. He did not then care like Newman for 'the intellectual tone of society', and he deeply distrusted the notion dear to Newman of 'cultivating the public mind'. The ideal of the gentleman fostered by Newman's liberal scheme of study could interest Tolstoy no more than it did the Russian radicals. He would have considered Newman as remote from realities as the educational theorists he was to meet in Europe.

Tolstoy maintained that the peasants would always resist efforts made from above to educate them. He believed that all they wanted for their children was the most elementary of skills – reading, writing and arithmetic. As to what they should read, he held by the Bible (meaning the Old Testament), and by folk tales and legends. It scandalised Chernyshevsky, whom Tolstoy hoped in vain to win over to his views, that in an otherwise wholly libertarian school he was prepared to enforce the teaching of religion. And from this followed a recommendation equally abhorrent: the teachers should not be graduates, village sextons would do better.

As becomes all too plain from an article of 1874, when Tolstoy had entered into dispute with the pedagogues, the kind of school he wanted was in radical eyes a nursery of superstition. However much he insisted on letting the children decide whether they would come to school or stay out if other interests or duties called, his proposed curriculum could scarcely have been more restrictive. He had turned his back upon all current thinking about education. The *Primer* for schoolchildren which he wrote and published in the early 1870s set out to nullify the tendentious teaching approved by the radicals. Rather than trying to 'develop' his pupil, as modern theory prescribed, the teacher should concentrate on the rudiments. Tolstoy entrenched himself in the old pieties: he declared that popular beliefs about the structure of the world, however ludicrous these might appear to the scientist, made sense for the peasant child. They were not to be driven out by lessons in abstract physics based very likely on shallow notions about the subject. Tolstoy stood by the countryman's deeply ingrained prejudices, and against the doctrinaire incompetence of a teacher from outside.

In *Hard Times* (1854) Dickens had ridiculed the educational practice of the utilitarians. Gradgrind on visiting his school is appalled to find that a girl who has spent her whole life with horses cannot describe one in the approved technical terms:

'Quadruped. Graminivorous. Forty teeth, namely twenty-four grinders, four eye-teeth, and twelve incisive', with the rest of the rigmarole. And similarly Russian theorists considered it their duty to instruct the child about 'real objects'. They assumed that he came to them with nothing whatsoever in his mind, which they must imprint with the truths of modern science. So the teacher must introduce his pupils to the idea of spatial relations. He explains the terms *over* and *under* (not, one would have supposed, hitherto unknown to them) with reference to the blackboard, its easel and tray. Tolstoy counterattacked by exposing a genuine ignorance on the teacher's part. Can he, as the children easily can, tell what kind of wood the blackboard is made from? Has he ever looked at a kitten or a hen with the close attention they give? Does he share their infallible sense of what is false? And by what right does he presume to 'develop' their minds?

Therefore Tolstoy recommended looking for somebody from the village itself to become the teacher. He accepted the view of the German populist Wilhelm Riehl, a well-known sociologist and cultural historian, that the people always liked rural teachers best. What really mattered was for the man to be 'simple and Russian'. As Arbiter of the Peace Tolstoy had been called upon to find teachers for the village schools of his district. In 1862 he recruited a number of university students sent down for political activity. This might have earned him the respect of the radical camp, had he not seized the opportunity to detach these young men from their philosophy. He wrote gleefully in his letters that they arrived with the conviction that the Bible was all rubbish, but contact with the people soon made their 'quasi-liberal nonsense . . . melt away like wax before a flame' (L 159). Within a week, he claimed, everyone one of them had burned the manuscript of the revolutionary thinker Herzen that he had brought in his baggage.

Tolstoy believed that education should be framed to answer questions arising from the child's experience, and the child for him, as we have seen, was a peasant. In this way his thinking about education anticipated the general position he would take some twenty years later, when the patriarchal peasant became the measure of all things. He wanted the school to be domestic, intimately connected with the child's home, and grounded in his daily concerns. The child was not to have his beliefs upset. He must be confirmed in sound morality. Whatever the teacher showed him must make sense to a simple understanding, and respond to practical needs. One critic protested of the *Primer* that Tolstoy too readily assumes 'nature was designed for the benefit of man and represents no more than an extensive property'. His emphasis on the useful and his impatience with speculation prove once more Tolstoy's inveterate eighteenth-century turn of thought.

Chernyshevsky could not refrain from pointing out that Tolstoy's 'pedagogic wisdom' took no account of modern developments. He rudely compared him with some half-educated assessor at a country court who would be hopelessly out of his depth as lawgiver, without any real knowledge of jurisprudence or acquaintance with contemporary thought on these matters. Tolstoy did indeed make a poor showing in 1874 when he tried to convince the experts that his own method of teaching children to read was better than theirs. He was always prodigiously self-reliant, and suspicious of what he held to be the prevailing misconceptions. Chernyshevsky's taunt, however, failed to reckon with the compensating virtue in Tolstoy's 'semi-literate' approach: his refusal to lose sight of the real situation in the villages.

Tolstoy's critics could not doubt that the measures he advocated were an outright attack upon the intelligentsia. In a reply to Chernyshevsky's strictures he turned his fire on the universities. All they did was to produce 'liberals of a certain pattern' who 'were not needed by the people'. He wrote at a moment ill-judged for such polemics. The authorities were starting a wave of repression, and when the article appeared Chernyshevsky was in prison and the *Contemporary* had been suspended. Tolstoy's intervention made him the blundering ally of the very same government that in July of this year, 1862, carried out a police raid at Yasnaya Polyana, in its owner's absence and much to his indignation.

The years of teaching gave no less to Tolstoy than to his

pupils. In a letter of 1863 he wrote, 'I'm glad that I passed through this school; this last mistress of mine was a great formative influence on me' (L 182). It is the effect of such unconstrained intimacy with peasant children upon his thinking in general that matters here. We are not judging Tolstoy as an educator: he was a writer, and the school at Yasnaya Polyana interested him only so long as it nourished his creative powers. Much though he enjoyed and profited by the exchanges with his pupils, one of whom said later in life 'we grew as close to Lev Nikolayevich as a cobbler's thread is to wax', Tolstoy had no mind to continue with the school when its usefulness to himself was at an end. In this way the experience resembled that of writing a novel. Once lived through, it no longer engaged him, and new interests supervened. Those, however, who make teaching their career have to accept that much of the work must be repetitive.

The most rewarding hours for Tolstoy and the children seem to have been those in which he told them stories, and later got them to write stories too. Much of what he expected to succeed with his audience when read aloud fell flat: *Robinson Crusoe*, Pushkin's prose tales (which he had formerly admired and would return to with no less enthusiasm) and the *Iliad* in the well-known verse translation by N.I. Gnedich (1830). He was always ready to accept the children's verdict as final. If their strong sense of logic found an incident in Homer to be absurd, then Homer must be abandoned. So too with the lyric poetry of Pushkin and the music of Beethoven. It was now clear to him that they ministered to a sick taste: the ballads and songs of the people were superior to the work of either. The peasant children gave him a criterion for the real, his constant preoccupation.

It was the same with their history lessons. Tolstoy quickly perceived that stories about the Pharaohs or medieval Russia in the time of the appanage principalities meant nothing to them. What wholly absorbed their minds and could be told by him to a breathless audience was the events of the year 1812 when the Russian people repulsed Napoleon.

Two of the boys, Fed'ka and Syomka, impressed him by

their ability to compose stories. Tolstoy would give his class a proverb to write about: they must illustrate it by a story of popular life to fit the theme. To get them going he suggested the characters and situation. These two boys, especially Fed'ka, took up the challenge with extraordinary confidence. Soon Tolstoy found he was acting merely as their scribe and occasional prompter. The fourth issue of the journal *Yasnaya Polyana* contained the story they wrote, its first page by Tolstoy seeming to him, when compared with their development of the rest, 'like a fly in milk'.

The whole experience was intensely moving. It gave him an ecstatic pleasure not unmixed with feelings of guilt, as though in some way he had 'profaned the pure primal innocence' of a peasant boy's soul. He saw himself as a kind of voyeur who peered into the glass hive of bees at work. Fed'ka's instinctive sense of proportion, the economy of the boy's art and his unerring selection of detail, amazed him. When a peasant in the story was described, at Tolstoy's suggestion, as putting a fur coat on, Fed'ka at once insisted it should be a woman's fur coat. From this masterly stroke (for such Tolstoy judged it to be) one was able to imagine the whole scene: the peasant 'feeble' and 'narrow-chested'; the woman's fur coat on a bench the first thing that came to hand; and then 'all the winter evening routine of peasant life' in the hut, when the man sits by rushlight, and the women move in and out on their errands, water-carrying or tending the cattle. So Fed'ka could reveal 'that outward disorder of peasant life, where no single person has clearly assigned clothing and no single thing its assigned place'.

It astounded him that a half-educated peasant boy should outstrip the artistry of Goethe. By allowing Fed'ka the freedom to write as he pleased Tolstoy had brought about the appearance of work unlike anything in the whole of Russian literature.

Perhaps only a reader with Tolstoy's insight could discover so much in a gifted child's writing. His conclusions are fully in the spirit of Rousseau, whose 'great utterance' he invokes, 'firm and true as a rock', in his account of the episode. 'Man is born perfect', and at his birth he embodies the harmonious union of truth, beauty and goodness. To this ideal state the peasant boy stands much nearer than those who aspire to teach him. They can only learn from his natural wisdom, just as the author of *Childhood* forgot his own success in literature and recognised the superiority to himself as a story-teller of the eleven-year-old Fed'ka.

The school at Yasnaya Polyana had done two things for Tolstoy. It had given him a special understanding of the Russian people through their children, and, as Eykhenbaum points out, it did eventually restore him to literature. The article 'Who Should Teach Whom To Write?' (1862), summing up the most valuable lesson for him of the school, is a declaration that shows where his deepest concerns lay.

4 The making of *War and Peace*

Tolstoy was at work on *War and Peace* from 1863 until 1869. A year before starting it he had married Sofya Behrs, sixteen years his junior, and had now become, as he wrote in the autumn of 1863, 'a husband and father, who is fully satisfied with his situation' (L 182); and never more conscious of his powers, intellectual and moral, and of the freedom to use them. He was totally the writer again, and lost to the village children as their teacher. He may a little have exaggerated his happiness. Earlier in that year he had talked of re-enlisting in the army to help put down the alarming Polish insurrection against Russian rule, which had the moral support of Britain, France and Austria. The coldness and scepticism of Prince Andrey in the novel might suggest that Tolstoy's intellect was not wholly satisfied with domestic bliss.

His first intention had been to write about the Decembrists, the enlightened members of the nobility who had staged a revolt on the death of Alexander I in 1825. Those surviving in 1856 were allowed to come back from their Siberian exile. Tolstoy meditated a contrast between these reformers, of his father's generation and class, and the 'new men' of the 1850s. Chernyshevsky had published in 1863 his treatise-novel *What Is To Be Done?*, dramatising (if that is the word for it) free love and collective enterprise. The book would have an immense appeal to young Russians for many years to come: Lenin was among its most devoted readers. Tolstoy attacked Chernyshevsky's scheme of life in the desk-drawer comedy, *An Infected Family*. He was fully alerted to the defence of marriage and the family as the corner-stone of civilisation. His novel was to celebrate the domestic scene of his immediate ancestors, whom he was 'positively glad to remember'.

The earliest version gave the foreground to peace; it was the fortunes of several aristocratic families that interested Tolstoy. He had thought of entitling the work *All's Well That Ends Well*.

However, once he reached the campaign ending in Austerlitz the balance was changed. War, quite lately central to his own experience, now demanded more attention. His first idea of a family novel on the English pattern was modified, to become the historical epic we know, in which large philosophical issues would be raised. But the completed *War and Peace* still has its very important domestic side. Further, it remains a 'comedy' at least in the sense that Dante used the term for his great poem, since it closes in triumph, and in various kinds of moral victory for the main characters. *War and Peace* certainly 'ends well'. So does Prince Andrey; and in other ways Pierre, Nikolay, his sister Marya and Natasha. The three cardinal virtues in Tolstoy's scheme – simplicity, goodness and truth – have prevailed. *War and Peace* could fittingly have borne the title of his last novel, *Resurrection*.

The conflict of 1812 necessarily came to dominate the novel, and brought to a focus all its concerns. Tolstoy like other novelists was interested in the lives of individual men and women, and every character stands out in full singularity. But always he notes them in relation to the group, the family. He likes to show the revealing similarities between members of the same family: Andrey's hauteur and dryness, received from his father; Hippolyte's face in its imbecility presenting a debased version of his sister Hélène's classical beauty. And Tolstoy attends to the moral assumptions, the tacit understanding within a family. He sees a regiment as such a family unit; more, Russia itself in the struggle with the French survives and triumphs because of its family cohesion. This reading of human life enables Tolstoy to discover an organising principle for his vast novel. And it sprang from his deepest conviction. John Bayley aptly summarises the basic issue of the war, as Tolstoy saw it, in terms of the opposition between 'family' and 'system'.

Hostile critics accused Tolstoy of idealising the old Moscow nobility. Theirs was a way of life – family, household, field labourers on the country estate, bound together by immemorial ties – which he thought valuable for Russia, holding it steady in times of confusion and danger. There is some truth in his contention that such patriarchal living – even with the injustices and huge inequalities on which it rested – did provide a community in which affections could grow between the people it involved. Pierre was deceived by the dream of his own benevolence, when touring the estates he had inherited, into supposing that these villagers really loved him (ii ii 10). But Tolstoy implies nothing specious in the scene of old Count Rostov dancing to the applause of his servants (i i 17). On a later occasion he shows how Natasha, brought up as she has been by a French governess, can display an instinctive feeling for the Russian dance (ii iv 7). An old-fashioned country upbringing has made her, as it did Pushkin's Tatyana, Russian at heart. When Tolstoy stresses the close relations within a household such as that of the Rostovs, he points to something that could exist, if we may call in the evidence of Sergey Aksakov in his memoirs of the same period.

Throughout the novel Tolstoy is at pains to separate the real from the artificial, the living from the dead. In such moral terms, starkly absolute, he always inclined to make his political judgements, and *War and Peace*, like most Russian writing of the 1860s, was inescapably political. For a while Andrey feels attracted by the ideas of the reformer Count M. M. Speransky, who at that time had the confidence of Alexander I. But Speransky's white puffy hands disconcert him (ii iii 6), and they are taken to be overwhelming evidence that their owner is morally deficient. Speransky's eyes debar any approach to intimacy. Their coldness is not like that which often comes over Andrey himself, whose whole expression can be transformed into the warmest sympathy when he meets Pierre. Speransky is presented as no more real than the members of high society in Petersburg.Whereas even a despotic and capricious old man from the other camp, Andrey's father, is redeemed by the sincerity of feeling which compels him when dying to ask for his daughter's forgiveness (iii ii 8). Tolstoy does not gloss over the incidental faults of those who have the sense of the matter in them. Countess Rostov can be quite ruthless in annulling Sonya's engagement to Nikolay, for the sake of her family (iv i 8). But when it comes to a confrontation, like that between the scheming Petersburg functionary Prince Vassily and the old prince over the attempt by the former to secure Marya for his worthless son Anatole, the genuine peremptorily routs the false (I iii 5).

This happens on a national scale when the Russian people drive out the French invader. The Russian victory is seen as grounded in moral superiority. Kutuzov, once the pursuit is in full swing, asks his troops to be magnanimous to the enemy. War must not deaden in Russian hearts that truth of feeling which has given them the strength to prevail.

The campaign of 1812 can spell the moral and spiritual recovery of individuals participating in it. Andrey and Pierre, the two principal seekers after truth in the novel, had argued in 1807 when crossing the river to Bald Hills about the meaning of life (II ii 12). They had not found any sure enlightenment. Andrey was to be saved from his aridity of spirit by falling in love with Natasha's youthful grace and spontaneity, until she fails him. During the year of separation imposed by Andrey to please his father she becomes infatuated with Anatole, and Andrey returns to the desert. Pierre, at length disillusioned with Freemasonry, had tried to smother his questionings in the comfortable routine of Moscow life. Borodino sends a revelation to them both. Andrey, fatally wounded, learns a new love, such as T. S. Eliot described in *Little Gidding*, that calls for 'detachment / From self and from things and persons'. Pierre, taken prisoner by the French after their entry into Moscow, meets Platon Karatayev, whose every act and word express that same detachment, with a benevolence as intrinsic to him as the perfume to the flower.

Platon, a little peasant conscripted for the army, beguiles Pierre at their first meeting, under arrest (IV i 12,13). His movements are effortlessly right, his speech is loving and inconsequential, his attention to others intimate but momentary. Long after the guards have shot him as a straggler, he continues to illustrate for Pierre 'all that is Russian, good and round'. Such 'roundness' betokens a nature worn smooth by life, that has no significance but as part of a far greater whole it recognises instinctively. It is like the drops in Pierre's dream after the death of Platon, coalescing into a globe, the world. When Tolstoy calls it peculiarly Russian he appears to get support from the speculations of a modern critic, Andrey Sinyavsky, who has opposed the roundedness of Russian church architecture to Gothic angularity, the soft flesh as against the hard bone. The critic N. N. Strakhov (for many years Tolstoy's close friend and consultant) found Karatayev's 'spiritual beauty' to be 'astonishing, beyond all praise'. He declared that it put into the shade every other attempt to portray the 'spirit and strength' of the Russian people.

Pierre's life is utterly changed by this meeting. Natasha when they are married knows that the test of her husband's projects for Russia must be whether Platon would have approved. This blessed simpleton (who puts a heavy strain upon our credulity) takes on a surprisingly large resonance in the spiritual drama of *War and Peace*. To Pierre, prostrated by witnessing the execution of prisoners, he gives back the sense of 'life's joy and robustness'. But his significance is finally to be measured in juxtaposing him with Kutuzov, who shows a similar disregard for logic, and as happily contradicts himself, allowing the ratiocination of military experts to pass over his head. Kutuzov, although physically feeble, aged and drowsy, proves the ideal leader for Russia in the campaign that will destroy the myth of Napoleon's invincibility. The commander-in-chief never meets Karatayev, and had he done so would scarcely have noticed him. But their attitude of submitting to the flow of life brings them together. Kutuzov puts aside all personal concerns in carrying out that duty for which the popular will has chosen him. He could not in his position display the imbecility of Karatayev, but holds on to a strong purpose. Contrast him however with Napoleon, and the gap between Kutuzov and Karatayev rapidly shrinks.

Napoleon is the false hero for Tolstoy, Kutuzov the genuine one. In Napoleon he sees a mind that never recognises its limitations, believes sincerely in its impostures, and runs always to rhetoric. Tolstoy seldom loses a chance of belittling Napoleon. There is indeed one apparently sublime moment at Austerlitz when, on horseback before his marshals on a sunlit hill overlooking the mists through which the Russians are blundering forward, Napoleon removes his glove as a signal for battle to begin (ɪ iii 14). But he is faced by an enemy whose morale has already been shaken by the awareness that the higher command lacks proper control. Elsewhere Tolstoy derides Napoleon for assuming that his gestures and proclamations could determine the course of history. Events take no account of Napoleon's plans. Kutuzov baffles him by simply ignoring the rules that were supposed to govern war. Borodino should have been a defeat for the Russians, who left the field. With growing uneasiness Napoleon comes to understand that the morale of his enemies is indomitable, while that of his own army has been exhausted.

Whatever Tolstoy may have owed for the perspective of his battle scenes to Stendhal's description of Waterloo in *La Chartreuse de Parme*, his own experience at Sevastopol gave them their peculiar force. He had learned that success or failure in battle depends ultimately on the individual soldier keeping his nerve and doing what the moment requires. From this he concludes that the general's part is not to interfere by making dispositions which, when his orders get through to the troops, will have become irrelevant. In the Austrian campaign of 1805 Andrey watches the Russian general Bagration in the field (ɪ ii 17). All that happens is determined by powers outside his control – by necessities of the local situation, by chance or by the decisions of his subordinates. Andrey admires Bagration's tact in letting it be thought the result accords with his intention. He does much for morale by his mere presence and bearing. One of Tolstoy's military critics, General Dragomirov, applauded this perception as particularly useful to commanders studying the art of war.

At a later stage in the writing of his novel, during 1868 and 1869, Tolstoy went on to develop an ambitiously conceived and much disputed theory of history. During the 1860s history had become a general interest in Russia, given more point by the half-centenary of Borodino in 1862. Another aspect of the debate concerned free will and necessity. Tolstoy when he began his novel had done all he could to ignore history as a force in men's lives. He wanted to show a timeless natural order, like that assumed by the eighteenth-century encyclopaedists. But the growing intrusion of war upon his narrative compelled him to formulate ideas on history.

He looked upon war as the great instrument of change. The immense upheaval in Europe brought about by the Napoleonic wars not surprisingly blinded him to the parallel and probably more significant process of the industrial revolution. His very strong feeling for Russia as a moral force (in which he resembled the Slavophils) made him respond passionately to the grandeur of the repulse to Napoleon on Russian soil. If only he could explain what resulted from Borodino this would lead to the understanding of what determines history. He could write about war with an authority denied to his opponents, who had been trained in the seminary rather than on the battlefield. And, as Isaiah Berlin has demonstrated, he found in the writings of the Savoyard political thinker, Count Joseph de Maistre (1754–1821) support for his views on war and his hostility to positivism.

In *War and Peace* Tolstoy, even though facing great difficulties when he tried to explain the historical process, could still trust in the operations of life, in nature and instinct. Right feeling is all. Kutuzov has been called upon to replace the admirable Barclay de Tolly who, being a German by origin, lacks rapport with the Russian people. Kutuzov never loses his touch in this respect: he understands the position not intellectually, but through being loyal to his Russian instincts. In this he shares the conviction of his men who, like Nikolay Rostov, never pause to cogitate but do what seems natural and right.

It is noticeable that nearly all Tolstoy's similes to explain the war are drawn from nature. At Austerlitz, indeed, the movement of the armies as it is set going reminds him of a clock mechanism; but this image serves to bring out the disproportion between such a convergence of forces and its result – after so much activity the hand on the clock dial of history no more than creeps forward. With the encouragement of a mathematically minded adviser, Prince S. S. Urusov, Tolstoy hoped it would be possible to evolve a science of history in terms of precisely calculated 'forces'. However, his strong visual imagination (and the reading of Homer) inclined him more to the use of graphic similes from rural life. So he will speak of 'the Russian nest' that has been 'ruined and destroyed' (IV i 10); of Moscow as a deserted bee-hive (III ii 20); of the ant-like return of its people (IV iv 14); and of the partisans gathering up the remnants of the French army like leaves from a withered tree (IV iii 3). Kutuzov during the rout of his enemies is compared with the market gardener who, once having driven out a beast that was trampling his crops, does not weary himself trying to beat it over the head (IV iii 19). That last image recalled a celebrated simile in the eleventh book of the *Iliad* for Ajax; but it also reveals a whole way of thinking. Kutuzov and the Russian army in unison with him show the patience and weather-eye of the countryman, who knows how to bide his time and work with the seasons.

Neither the historians nor the surviving witnesses of the 1812 campaign could accept Tolstoy's presentation. He had read deeply, but not widely; he was not above juggling with facts; and he claimed for the artist in his treatment of history a freedom denied to the scholar. For example, Tolstoy had read in Thiers of a Cossack prisoner who talked about the war to Napoleon 'with the most extreme familiarity' until shocked into silence on learning it was the Emperor he addressed. As a novelist Tolstoy could give the man a fictional identity and a story which reverse the effect of this anecdote. The Cossack is found to have been Lavrushka, an unsatisfactory serf handed over to Nikolay Rostov by Denisov. What the vainglorious Napoleon and his suite took for natural awe was 'really' the mother-wit of a Russian peasant who knew how to play on their credulity (III ii 7).

The most interesting case in the novel is that of Kutuzov. Here Tolstoy relies on popular myth, preferring what Urusov called 'factual tradition' to documents. Pushkin's historical study of the Urals revolt in the 1780s is less sympathetic to the peasant leader, Pugachov, than his novel *The Captain's Daughter* (1836). In the latter work Pushkin freely developed the image of Pugachov he had encountered when talking to people on the spot. Tolstoy in his turn wanted to shape a Kutuzov adequate to events that for his countrymen had now passed into legend.

A fiction so deeply considered imposes it own necessity. Marina Tsvetayeva defended the myth-making habit of another poet, Voloshin, by quoting his story of the little girl who wrote about a visit to the zoo: 'I have seen a lion – it wasn't at all like one.' Those who read of the historical Kutuzov will share her feelings.

Tolstoy's speculations on history begin to appear with the third volume of *War and Peace* and are given an unimpeded run in the second Epilogue. Many readers will have echoed Flaubert's cry of distress, reported by Turgenev: '*Il se répète! et il philosophise!*' Tolstoy was prepared for such criticism. But he explained to a friend and ally, the historical writer M.P. Pogodin, 'my ideas on the limits of freedom and necessity . . . are the fruit of a whole life-time's intellectual activity . . .' They could not be detached from an outlook on life in attaining which he thought he had won through to 'complete tranquillity and happiness' (L 218).

That these interpolations sit awkwardly in the novel is true. By rights they belong to another form of discourse, the philosophical treatise, in which Tolstoy was not the master he showed himself to be in fiction. Yet, however inappropriate the method, insisting when in a work of the imagination it should disclose, Tolstoy's argument does not leave his novel behind. It makes explicit the process of thought which had been working through the fiction. Flaubert would not admit such contamination of pure art. The manner is uncomfortably doctrinaire, but the doctrine itself grew out of Tolstoy's novel, and his decision to express it must be accepted as the decision of an artist.

We may regret the intrusion of earnest theorising into *War and Peace*. But it would be vain to separate the 'poetry' from the 'philosophy', as Croce wanted readers of the *Divine Comedy* to separate them. Writers with a metaphysical passion like Dante or Goethe or Tolstoy are driven to search for a unitary structure; they speculate on what they have observed; and Russian novelists in particular during Tolstoy's lifetime dealt boldly with ideas – they repeated themselves and they philosophised – because theirs was a culture in which ideas gained momentum as nowhere else. This was simultaneously the defect and the

supreme strength of the Russian novel. *War and Peace* has its ⌉
pages of pamphleteering. But they cannot be torn out, because | +
the argument is continuous. On every page lies the imprint of ⌋
the same evolving experience.

At this time he had newly discovered Schopenhauer, not
realising that many others, brought up on Hegel, were now
looking in the same direction. Tolstoy refused to accept the total determinism of contemporary scientists, their minds caught
fast in the fashionable disciplines of physiology and zoology.
For them everything was conditioned by the nervous system in
man as in frogs, rabbits and monkeys. Scientific observation led
to the doctrine of necessity, according to which progress, they
believed, was certain. Tolstoy, however, with support from his
reading of Schopenhauer, distinguished between the objective
necessity which the reason infers and the subjective aspect revealed to the consciousness never doubting its own freedom. He
formulated it in these terms: 'Reason expresses the laws of necessity. Consciousness expresses the essence of freedom.' Ap-
plied to the understanding of history this means that those who,
like Napoleon, put their confidence in reason alone are wholly
the prisoners of necessity. (And yet, as E. B. Greenwood points
out, Napoleon must bear the main responsibility for the slaugh-
ter at Borodino (III ii 38)). Kutuzov on the other hand or the
common soldier, accepting necessity without trying to impose
his will upon it, is free in the only way possible for a human
being. There can be no such thing as either total determinism
or total freedom. It was only when Pierre had been deprived of
all outward freedom as a prisoner of the French, and was subjected to almost entire privation, that he could recognise the
force of life within him. To feel you are alive is to feel free.
Without this irrational sense of freedom life would have no
meaning.

Edward Wasiolek has recently argued that the Russian word
for conscience, *soznaniye*, corresponding exactly to the French
conscience, would seem to stand, as used by Tolstoy, for a kind
of knowledge that merges with what it apprehends. He suggested that Tolstoy gave full weight to the prefix *so* (meaning
'with') before *znaniye* ('knowledge'). The characters feel most

free when they are wholly involved in some activity that dictates every move for them. Wasiolek cites the wolf hunt (II iv 4), in which dogs and men know their places and assigned tasks, so that the individual is perfectly in accord with his circumstances. Tolstoy's idea of a freedom which grows paradoxically out of coming to terms with necessity is not peculiar to him. Christians accept that God's 'service is perfect freedom'. Hegel spoke of freedom as the appreciation of necessity, and Engels quoted him with approval. It has become a commonplace of Marxist thought. Tolstoy, however, may have derived his conviction from an experience closer to the devout Christian's – the practice of his art. Poetic thinking is similar to religious obedience. And the novelist like the poet is bound to his inspiration. A story insists on telling itself in its own way, as Tolstoy found to his surprise in *Anna Karenina* when Vronsky made a sudden attempt at suicide (L 297).

What the writer has achieved by not trying in any way to distort or suppress his consciousness comes to have the look of inevitability. It is always hard to believe that trial and error played any part in Tolstoy's imaginative writing and that variants exist for scenes that could not, we feel, ever have been otherwise. But the writing of a novel such as *War and Peace* can indeed be compared with the waging of a campaign. Tolstoy at his best is another Kutuzov, allowing things to take their own course.

Henry James could not commend Tolstoy as an exemplary novelist. He saw in his work a surplus of undirected power which made for bad art. English critics would long regard Tolstoy as an elemental force, undisciplined and prodigious. The mirroring of all human life, on a vast scale, without artifice – that description of *War and Peace* cannot today be countenanced. It overlooks how selective, and how controlled for all the vast sweep, is Tolstoy's presentation of that 'wonderful mass of life' which James thought he had treated in so profligate a manner.

War and Peace does indeed celebrate life in its spontaneous forms. Tolstoy delights to show the happiness of a creature absorbed in the sufficiency of the moment, whether it is

Natasha at her first ball (ii iii 15–17), or Pierre with his new sense of exultation at being alive (iv ii 12), or Petya during his brief spell of military service, when everyone seems to him a hero and a comrade deserving his love (iv iii 7). The splendid confidence of the book is inseparable from a simplifying process which may be either its cause or its product. The Tolstoy of *War and Peace* came as near to knowing happiness and serenity as his demanding nature would ever allow. The contemplation of the year 1812 and of the part played in it by his ancestors released him temporarily from the burden of an oppressive conscience. In a war like that he describes, the justice of which from the Russian point of view cannot be denied, there is a kind of holiday of the spirit. Obligations are simpler and unquestioned, while fulfilment of the individual is more easily attained, as Nikolay knows.

Tolstoy could not fail to recognise the provisional and limited nature of this solution. He was not able to rest on the achievement of *War and Peace*. The polemical note in the second Epilogue warns his reader that the debate will continue, as it did in other forms but with a growing intensity.

5 Towards the crisis: *Anna Karenina*

It took time for the greatness of *War and Peace* to be acknowledged by Tolstoy's contemporaries, since the novel was not satisfactory either to radicals because of its overt political bias, or to conservatives because it had thrown some doubt on the patriotism of the nobility in 1812, and because Tolstoy seemed too much the 'nihilist'. Once again he withdrew from literature. Like other established writers of his generation Tolstoy had to recognise that the public was turning away from him.

The new decade brought unrest both at home and abroad. The Franco-Prussian war of 1870–1 and the Paris Commune gave notice that the European order had come under threat. In Russia social change began to jeopardise the dominance of the aristocracy. In 1874–5 two thousand young intellectuals went to the villages to bring political enlightenment and returned in disarray. The populist movement *Zemlya i Volya* (Land and Freedom) soon developed a terrorist wing, *Narodnaya Volya* (The People's Will: *volya* means both 'will' and 'freedom'), which in 1881 succeeded in assassinating the tsar.

With some reason, then, Strakhov in 1883, writing on three recent novels – Turgenev's *Virgin Soil* (1877, about the events of 1874–5 in the Russian countryside), *Anna Karenina* (1873–7) and Dostoyevsky's *The Brothers Karamazov* (1881) – could speak of the 'moral chaos' in Russian life they reflected.

Tolstoy was slow in finding his way to a new novel. After *War and Peace* he set to work on his *Primer*, and taught himself to read classical Greek. The superb economy of expression in Homer and Xenophon made him dissatisfied with his own writing. The tale *A Captive in the Caucasus* (1872) was designed for the *Primer*, approximating in its terse simplicity to the Greek ideal and so being more suitable for the plain reader. He began a novel about the epoch of Peter the Great. However, he could not animate it: the thought and manners of the age seemed too remote.

His decision to write on contemporary life was precipitated by a chance reading of Pushkin's prose tales. Two fragments, apparently related, told of a young married woman who shocked society by her passionate earnestness in a liaison that eventually became frustrating for herself and oppressive to her lover. Three years before Tolstoy had been interested in the idea of a society woman in that situation: the pity rather than the blame of it should be shown. His encounter with Pushkin's sketches at once got him going, and with an unwonted ease. Pushkin's control of tone, his unerring eye for proportion, and his directness held a particular appeal for Tolstoy. He cherished them as the marks of a civilisation in his own contentious time sadly outmoded. Latterly he had been ready to dismiss Pushkin's language as 'absurd' in comparison with popular speech. Now it seemed plain that Pushkin and Homer inculcated the same virtues of style (L 260).

The position of women was a topic much debated in those years; Tolstoy had long brooded on it. He was delighted to see Strakhov attack Mill's book *On the Subjection of Women* (1869). Another ally appeared in the younger Dumas, whose tract of 1872 *L'Homme-femme* upheld a husband's duty to form and discipline his wife. Should she prove incorrigible, he could even take it upon himself to end her transgressions by killing her. Tolstoy would allow no such drastic step to safeguard the husband's honour. His epigraph for *Anna Karenina*, 'Vengeance is mine; I will repay', leaves punishment to God working through the moral law.

Like *War and Peace* this novel altered in the writing. Certain features, however, would remain fixed. The heroine was always to throw herself under a train. When Anna in the moment before death shrinks from the oncoming wheels, 'something huge and relentless' drags her down (vii xxxi). Tolstoy added the phrase when making his final revision; but the idea had always been present. In an early draft the husband (a more likeable man than Karenin) seees her as possessed by the devil. Kitty views her in this light at the ball (i xxiii). With succeeding drafts Anna becomes more beautiful, a rarer person; but Tolstoy cannot forget that she menaces the family. He is deeply stirred by her sexuality, which transcends that of Hélène in *War and Peace* and expresses itself in her energetic movements and the warmth of her nature. Anna's love for Vronsky may seem to represent the triumph of genuine feeling over the falsity now manifest in her marriage. But Tolstoy is fearful of spontaneity in the form of sexual passion, and it leads to her downfall. He never loses sight of what he firmly believes to be her moral delinquency, which determines that she should merely escape from one form of self-deception into another. Anna as Vronsky's mistress cannot secure for herself either dignity or peace of mind (which are persistent concerns in this novel).

War and Peace had held Tolstoy's almost undivided attention as *Anna Karenina* could not. His dispute with the populist intelligentsia, arising out of the quarrel in 1874 with the pedagogues, made the original theme of his novel appear trivial and even repellent. Within less than two years he was feeling 'quite unable to tear myself away from living people' – the 'thousands of children' whose need for education was again worrying him – in order to concentrate upon mere fictional characters. For a long while he practically gave up the novel. However, quite early its scope had broadened to take in the story of Levin's courtship and his successful marriage to Kitty. Anna's predicament alone, however keenly felt, could not absorb Tolstoy's mental energies. The integrity of marriage greatly mattered to him. He could contain the dangerous appeal of Anna by showing a love that drew its strength from family obligations and social activity prescribed by custom. Thus Levin and Kitty must care for his dying brother Nikolay; thus Levin must work with his peasants, supervising and at times taking a hand himself; parenthood, stewardship of the land, maintenance of the ancestral home – all these duties helped to guarantee the marriage. Sexual passion (of which in their union we hear little, apart from Levin's jealousy of Vasenka Veslovsky (VI xiv)) is seemingly monopolised by Anna and Vronsky. The presence of Levin in the book was liberating for Tolstoy. The ever narrowing possibilities in Anna's life could now be offset by the spiritual growth of someone increasingly like the author.

Tolstoy could not carry on with the story of Anna until he

had found this means of bringing all his preoccupations to bear on the novel. Fiction must answer his needs even more directly than in *War and Peace*, or he could not see it as wholly serious. He told Fet in October 1875 when at last writing was again in full swing, that without proper 'scaffolding' it was hopeless for a novelist to go on (L 281). Until Levin's position (which was his own) had however tentatively been worked out, the agony of the heroine would merely distract him from more imperative claims. Once these had been brought into the scenario, he became free to contemplate the meaning of Anna's destruction, fully in command of himself.

His aloofness from public affairs was not complete. In 1873 he took action over the Samara famine, in 1874 he did battle with the pedagogues. Levin is alive to many topical issues. Through him Tolstoy struck out, as always, against whatever he considered to be unreal; the agitation for women's rights, which threatened the weakening of the marriage tie; the importance ascribed by liberals to a new organ of local self-government, the *zemstvo*; the pretensions of social philosophers like Levin's half-brother Koznyshev; and finally the Slavophil zeal for rescuing the Serbs from Turkey. On these and other questions such as the proper management of landed property Tolstoy takes his stand like any publicist. But *Anna Karenina* is not a novel in which ideas obtrude as they do with H. G. Wells and not seldom with Hardy. Tolstoy explained in a famous letter to Strakhov that the ideas there must be seen in their relationship to the whole design: 'If I were to try to say in words everything that I intended to express in my novel, I would have to write the same novel I wrote from the beginning.' The truth must be sought in what he called the 'endless labyrinth of connections' (L 296–7).

Anna Karenina is formally a more balanced work than *War and Peace*. Even the meditations of Levin at its close form part of the action. They could not be separated from his narrrative as were the passages on history in one edition of *War and Peace*. Tolstoy described the book when starting it as 'a novel, the first in my life'. It approximates in its development through contrast to *Middlemarch* (he admired George Eliot, but there is no positive evidence that he had read this book) and to *Madame Bovary* in its use, though much more sparing, of symbolism. It is more consciously planned on 'European' lines than any previous work by Tolstoy: the derivation from Pushkin, so well versed in the literature of Europe, would have strengthened this aim. Far from being an unruly representation of life as it happens before our eyes, *Anna Karenina* has been contrived with a deliberate artistry. Its organisation may be called in a broad sense musical. It works by cumulative statement, by repetition and counterpoint, by the alternation of tempo and mood. We could describe Tolstoy's procedure in terms of orchestration, which serves an elaborate matching of themes rather than the construction of a plot.

Dostoyevsky thought the novel old-fashioned, perceiving its continuity with Tolstoy's earlier fiction and with Pushkin. Anna's dilemma is that of Pushkin's heroine at the end of *Eugene Onegin* (1823–30), married to an elderly general who cannot stir her heart as Onegin does. Tolstoy re-opens the question – Tatyana in the last scene had pledged loyalty to her husband – but though his answer is different, he is working manifestly in the tradition of Pushkin and, as Eykhenbaum has said, his realism springs from a similar vision. *Anna Karenina* is the last and finest of the so-called 'gentry novels' written also by Turgenev, Goncharov and others. Dostoyevsky's point is not difficult to take. The same attitudes and concerns persist that were present in *War and Peace*. Levin's restlessness allies him to Andrey, his naïvety to Pierre; Karenin and Speransky are ostriches of a feather; Anna is temperamentally not far from Natasha; and the Shcherbatskys would see eye to eye on every important issue with the Rostov family. The old distinction is renewed between the real and the phantasmal. Once Levin with his brusque realism had made an entrance, Karenin could be despatched to the party of those who wall themselves in with abstractions. He becomes a functionary whose function is meaningless and prevents any emergence of the natural man in him, such as appears briefly when he keeps visiting the nursery to look at Anna's child by Vronsky (IV xix). He cannot sustain the peace of mind that follows his impulse to forgive the lovers.

Fear of public opinion continues to rule his life, and he declines into a specious pietism shared with Countess Lydia Ivanovna. Alexey Karenin cannot be detached from the false milieu in which he lives. To a certain degree this is true of the other Alexey, his rival Vronsky.

For many readers, and notably for Lawrence, the inadequacy of Karenin justifies Anna in leaving him. They condemn Anna for her lack of resolution alone: she ought to have taken up the challenge of a hypocritical society, confident in her rightness. Tolstoy has complicated the matter by causing the reader to share Anna's repugnance for her husband's physical being. There seems to be no appeal against the implied moral judgement in such an instinctive response. When Anna cannot respond to a nobly forgiving Karenin because his clammy hand offends' her, these critics find here a fatality that may not be questioned. Varenka, the young woman of good works whom Kitty meets in Germany, is described as 'a flower without scent' (II xxx). Unlike Princess Marya she has nothing to redeem her plainness; no 'unrestrained flame of vitality' plays in Varenka, whose goodness lacks spontaneity. Instinctive feeling has led Tolstoy into a form of determinism: physical character, it seems, is fate.

The life that overflows in Anna does not of itself make her admirable. Eykhenbaum compared her with a sacrificial figure of protest, Katerina, the heroine of A. N. Ostrovsky's play *The Thunderstorm* (1860). Katerina is oppressed by the cramping traditional ways of her husband's family in a small town on the Volga, and when she cannot escape with her lover, she chooses death. Anna also is too large and generous in feeling to suit the society in which Karenin moves with such satisfaction. She brings herself to defy its conventions when, as Vronsky's mistress, she tries to outface the disapproval of her former friends at the opera (v xxxiii). But this act of bravado aims merely to regain her a place in that world of fashion which had imprisoned her spirit.

The affair with Vronsky, though it frees her from the insincerities in marriage with Karenin of which Dolly had been aware, does not allow Anna to face the truth of her situation until it is too late. Dolly interprets the way she screws up her eyes as a sign of this (VI xxi). In Italy she had pretended that her happiness was complete and that she did not feel the loss of her son Seryozha (V viii). With the few friends that visit her after the return to Russia, she cannot be entirely natural, any more than with Vronsky, whose interest she dare not forfeit. When Levin finally meets her Anna exerts all the charm of which she is capable to win him over. With the aid of Mikhaylov's dazzling portrait she becomes a seductress, even though doing this to establish her own position with Vronsky (VII x). Tilt the balance a little more openly, and the scene would resemble that in *Resurrection* (II xxiv) when Nekhlyudov responds to the flirtatious advances of Mariette whose husband's influence he needs.

Anna Akhmatova protested that Tolstoy built this novel upon 'physiological and psychological falsehood'. It outraged her that the heroine when married to dull Karenin should have been entirely virtuous, and once she had gone off with Vronsky should behave like a prostitute. Akhmatova suspected that Tolstoy had given in to the prejudice of his wife and aunts. Certainly to have exposed Anna to the fearful consequences of her adultery argues in Tolstoy a set purpose and a thesis. It becomes very clear that he finds her lawless passion deeply disturbing. A conscience as strict as Tolstoy's must have been aware that the long drawn-out imagining of this beautiful woman's predicament was a kind of infidelity to his own wife: hence the outbursts of disgust with the novel. He cannot be easy about Anna because of her sexuality. It has been noted that in this novel (long before *The Kreutzer Sonata*) he associates sexual passion with murder. Vronsky after finally possessing Anna contemplates her with the horror of a killer for the victim's corpse (II xi). They are both overcome by intolerable shame. Akhmatova was at least right in thinking that Tolstoy is not an impartial judge of Anna's case.

Yet he cannot be said to have falsified the consequences of what she did, in that society and given the nature of Vronsky himself. He is another Nikolay Rostov, decent and conventional, and quite unequal to the demands of her greater intensity and seriousness. Vronsky had been entirely at home in the regiment. The army gave him an object in life, a career and self-respect. After her suicide he returns to soldiering, in a desperate, almost cynical way: at least he can serve some purpose again, though as a man he is a ruin (VIII v). Anna had left him no option but to dabble in art, and then in politics; their grand establishment in the country was a fraud. Lawrence called on them to create 'a new colony of morality'. But it had no chance of being realised by two people whose relationship was increasingly flawed through Anna's almost insane jealousy. At the end, by a logic that it is impossible to resist or to brand as 'psychological falsehood', Anna is doomed to sink into the vacuity and terror of an existence without meaning. Once Tolstoy had set up her situation of a marriage subtly wrong and not capable of satisfying Anna's instinct for life, ultimate ruin must follow. Either she goes with her lover, and forsakes her son for an illusory happiness; or she stays with Karenin reconciling herself to what on Tolstoy's terms is a deadly falsehood.

In the moral system of *Anna Karenina* the heroine, having devoted her abundant gifts for life to a selfish purpose, is done away with. On the other hand Stiva, an adept at living for himself, continues to charm his friends and to prosper. Tolstoy in one sense lets him off lightly; but Stiva, though less obviously than Levin's half-brother, the philosopher Sergey Ivanovich, belongs to the limbo of the unreal. He resembles the worldly-wise Beletsky of *The Cossacks* in the way he brings others to approve of his unashamed self-indulgence; and Tolstoy may be a little fascinated by him, as more strongly he is by Anna. Yet Stiva, so comfortable in that society from which Anna is banished, must be judged with it. When the book ends he has procured a further lucrative job for himself. The incident is not thrown into relief like the award of the Legion of Honour to Homais the chemist, recorded in the final sentence of *Madame Bovary*. But the import is similar. A world of which the author is severely critical looks after its own.

Levin and Stiva had been friends in youth, but now they each with a pitying tolerance regard the life of the other as unreal. For Levin the question of what constitutes the real, the genuine, is tormenting. As the story develops Tolstoy invests more and more of the book's positive significance in this character. Implicitly he is contrasted with Anna throughout – but it is principle rather than force of circumstances that sets him at odds with society. His opposition is unweakened by any wish to compromise. Thus he remains a free agent. Levin's marriage occurs at the time of her elopement to Italy; Levin's crisis of despair follows upon hers, but the reasons for it are different, and the outcome is contrary. He and Anna dominate the novel: they are almost equivalent forces, but moving in disjunction to ends that cannot be reconciled. With Levin is connected the stability of marriage and home; Anna's severance from that stability begins on the railway, in search of happiness she becomes a nomad, and her death takes place on a departure platform. But for Levin the whole of life is centred upon his estate. It had been his ambition to raise a family in the old wooden house inherited from his parents: marriage should be the main business of life (i xxvii). Once settled with Kitty he feels like a ploughshare that cuts deeper and deeper into the earth (viii x).

Levin still exemplifies the insight that Tolstoy had made central to *War and Peace*. By confining himself to the tasks of the moment, and serving his own needs rather than those of mankind (which are impossible to grasp), he does always the necessary thing. The public interests of Sergey Ivanovich – first local government, the *zemstvo*, then the Serbian war – do not concern Levin. Being a landowner he is compelled to think about agricultural problems. At the house of the liberal Sviyazhsky where they discuss these, he feels respect for the old diehard who does that rare thing – speaks his mind (iii xxvii). This is Levin's own habit, first revealed when he interrupts the professor talking about philosophy with Sergey Ivanovich, by putting a blunt question that bears on his personal anxieties rather than their debate (i vii). In this way he proceeds throughout the novel, with a peasant-like obduracy that lets him claim to be one of the people, sharing their distrust of the learned and their prejudice in favour of custom.

The spectrum of Levin's experience includes courting and marriage, the death of a brother, the birth of a child. Through him Tolstoy pursues that theme so much favoured in the eighteenth century, the quest for happiness or, as Johnson terms it in *Rasselas*, 'the choice of life'. And Levin's impatience with sophistry and with what he believes to be illusion is thoroughly in the spirit of Johnson. He is a rational thinker who makes his appeal to experience, the great dissolvent of predetermined schemes. Sergey Ivanovich discovers their fragility when, instead of proposing to Varenka as he had intended, he finds himself conversing with her about mushrooms (VI v). Here the genuine self, the self of unacknowledged experience, subverts the constructions of the intellect. Karenin, who hides wherever possible behind abstractions, is not able to face a woman's tears. The superiority of Levin over these intellectuals is that however unschooled his thinking may be it deals pertinaciously with the findings of experience.

The most intractable experience for Levin is one that neither marriage nor the safely enclosing routine of the estate can drive from his thoughts. The death of Nikolay, even though Kitty's pregnancy comes like new grass to cover a devastated area, has the effect of almost paralysing Levin. When some time before he had met Nikolay and could tell what was coming, the only way out of the darkness seemed to be in work – the recourse of many nineteenth-century agnostics to save their sanity (III xxxii). But now that the actual moment arrives, and he and Kitty must endure the long ordeal of Nikolay's dying, though her nearness brings some comfort, the horror he feels is stronger than ever (v xx). Whereas in *War and Peace* Tolstoy could make death tolerable (partly because in war it is so general, partly because it seems to fit into an alternating rhythm with life, as war does to peace), here it stands out starkly. The final chapter of the episode is unique in bearing a title: 'Death'.

The shock leaves him helpless to find any point in his existence. He has a long struggle to keep away from suicide. The misery of that condition was Tolstoy's own; it takes over the final part of the novel. Relief is contrived for Levin through an encounter with peasant wisdom. He has been showing Fyodor on the farm how to work a new threshing machine. In the casual talk that follows Fyodor becomes his instructor about the meaning of life. A man must 'live for his soul' and 'remember

God' (VIII xi). The precept blinds him with its light. Henceforward he will be master of his life, even if faults of character remain (VIII xix). Levin's illumination is not so drastic in effect as St Paul's on the road to Damascus. He stops short of calling it faith: rather it is a feeling which his sufferings have imperceptibly brought about, and which is now secure. He has achieved a new orientation. The world has once more become right. In the last chapter he watches the summer lightning blot out the stars, and every time they return as if thrown back by an accurate hand.

Why did those few words from Fyodor bring Levin such reassurance? They did so because they ended his separation from the instinctive feeling which the peasants have, and which is shared by women, as Kitty proves. It may be significant that Levin, just before the revelation, had taken Fyodor's place at the threshing machine. He becomes his associate in work, and the process by which he arrives at illumination may be compared with that of his earlier mowing with the peasants (III iv). He has only to lose his self-awareness as a perplexed intellectual by submitting to union with the people among whom belief is real and steadfast.

There is a certain parallel between the end of this novel and that of *War and Peace*. The action, though ostensibly complete, pauses before new developments. Anna's account has been closed, and Vronsky's almost so. But for Levin there remains an indefinite future, and the insight he has gained from Fyodor is to be tested in the years before him. *Anna Karenina*, like its predecessor, closes with the seeking out of a position. But Levin's thinking is done in the conditions of his particular life – Kitty breaks into his exaltation to ask if he will see to the new washstand for Sergey Ivanovich's room. Never again would Tolstoy work on this scale with such attention to the complexities, or hold contraries in balance so sensitively, as he did in *Anna Karenina*, surely his greatest novel.

6 Tolstoy and religion

Two years after the last instalment of *Anna Karenina* came out, Tolstoy began to write his *Confession* (1879–82). The long threatening crisis of belief which had left its mark on the second half of the novel now overwhelmed him. Throughout the 1880s he would be active in demolishing the assumptions and attitudes that bound him to his own class, and to family life on which he had relied for happiness. The thirty years still before him were to bring much unease and anguish.

The *Confession* is a powerful work, deeply serious but not wholly to be trusted. Like many converts to a new way of life Tolstoy overstresses the blindness and depravity of his unregenerate past, and also misrepresents the positions he had then held. Thus he claims to have been at one with the liberals in accepting (with only occasional doubts) the idea of progress. He made out that he wrote simply for money and applause, and to avoid the real moral issues before him. All he could see was the hollowness of his achievement. To contemplate *Anna Karenina* now filled him with shame.

In the *Confession* Tolstoy speaks of spiritual discomfort having grown in him like a disease, at first revealed by transient symptoms but gradually mastering the whole organism. The process is realised in his finest tale of the decade, *The Death of Ivan Ilyich* (1886). This describes the fatal illness that cuts off a complacent and unremarkable civil servant from the life that had been his, forcing him at last to recognise its vanity and selfishness. He is left alone with the dreadful prospect of death. It had been the final agony of Tolstoy's own brother Nikolay that gave such intensity to the description in *Anna Karenina* of his namesake's last days and hours. A letter of 1860 to Fet just after the event is harrowing in its despair (L 141). If there is no survival after death, he concludes, then life becomes the most cruel of deceits.

In the *Confession* Tolstoy brings himself to confront the terror of annihilation. He had suffered in 1869 his so-called 'Arzamas misery' at an inn of that place. *The Memoirs of a Madman* (1884) describe this 'vastation', to use the elder Henry James's term for a seizure of his own. James's son William, the psychologist, diagnosed the case of Tolstoy as 'pathological depression', leading to 'loss of appetite for all life's values', with a consequent 'effort for philosophic relief'. Schopenhauer taught that peace could be attained only by renouncing life and its illusions. But the 'will to live', in which Schopenhauer saw the root of human suffering, was too strong in Tolstoy for him to acquiesce in this doctrine. Moral activity alone could satisfy him.

He tells how very gradually 'the strength of life' came back, when he returned to the beliefs of his earliest childhood. As Levin had done, he sought help in his perplexities from the common people. He longed to stifle the voice of his rationality, even though the faith he envied was inseparable from superstitions. For a time he strove to accept the dogmas and rites of the Orthodox Church. But a growing uneasiness could not be stilled. He was revolted by the Church's exclusive claim to truth, by its intolerance, by its readiness to support war in the national interest. Finally he was driven to make his own study of the scriptures, resulting in two declarations of independence: *A Criticism of Dogmatic Theology* and *A Translation and Harmony of the Four Gospels*.

Tolstoy's inspiration would always remain the Sermon on the Mount (Matthew 5–7). This he accepted as the most profound moral utterance in all human history. But Jesus was not the Son of God, nor had he risen from the dead, nor had his death on the cross atoned for the sins of mankind. The 'sons of God' were all those who fulfilled the commandments of Christ. The life that is perfectly moral becomes everlasting. N. A. Berdyayev, contributing with other Christian apologists to a symposium on Tolstoy's religion in 1912, wrote disparagingly of his 'Anglo-Saxon religiosity.' Tolstoy did indeed respond sympathetically to Matthew Arnold's *Literature and Dogma* (1873). 'Half of M. Arnold's thoughts are my own,' he once stated. I rejoice to read him' (L 382). Tolstoy demanded of religion that it should be altogether simple and clear. Berdyayev was scandalised by his contempt for the miraculous, the least concession to which he feared would destroy that simplicity and clarity. Tolstoy felt a hunger for the certitudes of religion, but whether he should be termed essentially a religious thinker is open to dispute. Above all he was concerned with finding an unassailable rule of conduct. The creed he promulgated has its place among the great moral systems, like Confucianism, rather than with the many forms trinitarian Christianity has taken. His allegiance to Christ was very real, but only to Christ as a moral teacher, not as a living presence revealed in contemplation, or a redeemer, or the incarnation of the divine. Maude relates that Tolstoy used to pray; but he does not approach the trembling submission, the awe and humility of Johnson, who suffered from the same dread in the face of mortality.

Berdyaev protested that the Tolstoyan doctrine led to 'the impoverishment of life', and a similar complaint was made by the Marxist critic G. V. Plekhanov, who pointed out that the morality Tolstoy derived from the Sermon on the Mount took the form of a series of prohibitions, having at their heart, from Christ's admonition 'Resist not evil', the agonisingly difficult ideal of non-violence. Tolstoy in his religious system as in all else demands the uncomplicated. A life that constantly denies itself any compromise with the world aspires to be uncomplicated. Tolstoy the sensualist becomes Tolstoy the ascetic; but not, as Berdyaev noted, one in the tradition of Francis of Assisi from whose followers Dante derived the image of the saint joyfully taking poverty as his bride. Berdyaev connects Tolstoy with an altogether different tradition – that of the Russian intellectual with populist leanings who 'simplified himself' for the people's good. And this bleak self-denial was an unlovely thing for Berdyaev, since it entailed an assault upon aesthetic values and metaphysics and upon mysticism, to which Tolstoy himself had been prone in his days of celebrating the harmony between nature and unspoilt man.

The religious mind is never, one would suppose, hostile to mystery or impatient with paradox. Those who, like Berdyaev and his associates, had rediscovered Christianity for themselves at the beginning of this century looked to Dostoyevsky rather than to Tolstoy for the dramatisation of the Christian argument. Dostoyevsky too had that streak of nihilism which has often been discerned in Tolstoy. He too was at grips throughout his life with the prevailing positivism, and no more than Tolstoy could he altogether avoid its influence. Both have correctly been termed heretics, if only because of their stubborn self-reliance, and the demand for rational explanation which fuelled that 'furnace of doubt' from which Dostoyevsky's hosanna was raised, only to falter again, and which drove Tolstoy into an iconoclasm as savage as ever Puritan rage produced in the West. Tolstoy did indeed commit himself to an immense 'effort for philosophic relief', and the practical results of his teaching must be taken very seriously. But if the mark of a truly religious man is the awareness (to quote Eliot's *Ash Wednesday*) of 'our peace in His will', Tolstoy was not such. It would seem that he never achieved any lasting peace; and the will that is manifest in the later writings is Tolstoy's own will to impose a solution without final certainty.

He became increasingly opposed to Orthodoxy, once he could no longer feel it bound him to the beliefs of the common people. Tolstoy was drawn to the dissident sects of the Old Believers, who had refused to accept the reforms introduced into the Russian Orthodox Church two hundred years before; and his quarrel with the established church was violent and irreconcilable. It led finally to excommunication in 1901 by the Holy Synod, an act which, as his biographer Maude puts it, 'surprised the world'. It certainly distressed many Christians, and there were even those who felt that the Church in rejecting Tolstoy had itself gone into the outer darkness. Under its lay procurator appointed by the government, K. P. Pobedonostsev, it had become closely involved in secular politics, and part of the antagonism to Tolstoy's teaching arose from an awareness that its own interests were threatened by Tolstoy's condemnation of the existing State. The Orthodox Church had long been guilty of obscurantism and repression.

However, the scandal was not all on the Church's side. Tolstoy gave deep offence by his attack on its rites and ceremonies, in which he showed himself the heir of the French Encyclopaedists. Mention has already been made of Shklovsky's term 'making strange' (*ostraneniye*) to describe Tolstoy's favourite practice when he wants to compel a new vision of things. Thus Natasha visiting the opera finds she cannot submit to its illusion, and everything that happens on the stage affects her as meaningless (II v 9). Tolstoy strips away all the associations that custom has prescribed. His detachment may suggest that of an anthropologist, but unlike the latter he deliberately refrains from supplying the context in which the action becomes intelligible. Two notorious chapters of *Resurrection* (I xxxix, xl) describe a mass held for the convicts. Tolstoy begins with an intentionally crude account of the service – the priest in his peculiar and uncomfortable garb, the deacon's old strained voice, the inaudible and incomprehensible prayers, the unbelievable doctrine, and the strange practice of manipulating bits of bread put in wine to become the body and blood of God. We may recall Nikolenka's uneasiness at the behaviour of the grown-ups during the requiem for his mother in *Childhood*. Here, however, the suspicion of insincerity has become a rancorous conviction. Tolstoy abhors the holding of such a service to worship the God of justice and mercy in a prison chapel where the incongruity between word and deed is so shockingly clear. The caustic tone of his description equals that used by Swift in *A Tale of a Tub* (1704) to expose the 'ridiculous inventions of popery'. It attacks what the writer condemns as blasphemy in language that is itself blasphemous for those who treasure the forms of Christian worship, uncorrupted even by this dubious application. Tolstoy's moral wrath is understandable, but he expressed it in provocative terms that many Christians, however critical of the Orthodox Church, would naturally resent.

Unable, as S. N. Bulgakov complained in the 1912 volume, to accept the antinomies of the Christian gospel, Tolstoy persisted in his stubbornly heroic efforts to reduce everything to simplicity itself. He was determined to prove what Jesus had 'really' meant; to 'recover' the true Gospel from the narratives of the four Evangelists; to settle all questions and to call the world back to righteousness. Not surprisingly there is to be detected a note of arrogance, even of bigotry, in some of his pronouncements. Gorky, who sincerely admired Tolstoy, but was never quite comfortable with him, did not approve of his aspiration to saintliness when playing the role of 'our father the blessed boyar Lev'. It seemed to Gorky that Tolstoy's attitude as a teacher was coercive, and that he would have liked martyrdom to silence all criticism of his doctrine. Gorky sensed the unhappiness in Tolstoy – that restless dissatisfaction with himself that made him a troubled and sometimes impatient seeker right to the end.

According to Berdyayev, sin for Tolstoy 'was simply ignorance, simply a weakness in rational understanding of the law of the Father'. Violence and cruelty do appear in *The Power of Darkness* (1886), a harsh play about peasant life the title of which bears out Berdyayev's statement; and they are there in his account of a Caucasian tribal chief living by his own traditions, *Hadji Murat* (written between 1896 and 1904). Tolstoy, however, clung to a belief in man's natural goodness. The peasant boy Gerasim, who attends the dying Ivan Ilyich, feels an instinctive compassion and behaves towards him with true Christian charity. But if evil was generally for Tolstoy an aberration which could be corrected by living like the unspoilt peasants, in one important particular he did endow it with a malign energy. If Tolstoy ever cries out 'Get thee behind me, Satan', it is when he seeks to ward off the power of uncontrollable sexual passion. Gorky tells of his outburst declaring that 'the most tormenting tragedy for man' has always been 'the tragedy of the bedroom'.

Carnal temptation figures as the devil in a story of that name (1889), and again in *Father Sergius*, started the following year. Nekhlyudov's touchingly innocent love for Katyusha in *Resurrection* (1899) is ruined by his bestiality: the 'animal man' tramples upon the spiritual man. Tolstoy's most violent denunciation of the sexual instinct was made in *The Kreutzer Sonata* (1890). Pozdnyshev the narrator of his frenzied *crime passionel* – he murdered his wife on the suspicion of adultery – is evidently a psychopath, and one might hesitate to accept his views as Tolstoy's. But the Afterword proposes 'the ideal of complete chastity' even in marriage. Tolstoy acknowledges 'I was startled at my conclusions and did not wish to believe them'. The attempt to honour these in his own marriage was not successful and brought him much pain.

The Kreutzer Sonata is not the finest product of Tolstoy's conversion, nor is it typical of the later work except in its relentless drive to a dogmatic conclusion. Tolstoy should not be judged as a religious and moral thinker by this one extreme instance. But it is impossible to ignore the book, just as *Lady Chatterley's Lover* has to come into a final estimate of Lawrence. These novels are at least symptomatic of a less than perfect control, and the desire to prove is in both too evident.

Tolstoy's writings of the last thirty years, given their aim, are certainly impressive. The *Confession* argues its case with superlative skill. The utter simplicity and the heavy reiteration are weapons of rhetoric. As a master of perspicuous statement Tolstoy has no equal in Russian literature unless it be Pushkin. The hard clarity of the *Confession* is present not only in his many treatises – religious, moral and social – but in those works of fiction he still allowed himself to write. *The Death of Ivan Ilyich* demonstrates no less starkly than the *Confession* the futility of a life that has never weighed its significance in the light of death. *Master and Man* (1895) is supremely well realised – the deepening snow, the altering relations between the two men, the master's self-satisfaction that turns to panic and then to his uncharacteristically selfless act. *Father Sergius* is an acute study of spiritual pride overthrown by ill-guarded impulse. *The Kreutzer Sonata*, in its fierce obsessiveness much nearer to Dostoyevsky's writing than any other work by Tolstoy, states what is properly a clinical case with great accuracy. And *Resurrection*, the major undertaking of those years, though less subtle than *War and Peace* and *Anna Karenina*, goes deep into Nekhlyudov's dilemma when after many years he finds himself on the jury trying a girl whose downfall began with his seduction of her. The novel connects the prison world and high society, somewhat in the manner of Dickens during the 1850s. Though *Resurrection* is more schematic and less diversified then, say, *Little Dorrit*, the thrust of Tolstoy's criticism is equally strong.

In all of his writing, fictional or publicistic, after the crisis

Tolstoy shows no loss of power. Such occasional weaknesses as occur had their precedents in the earlier work. When Tolstoy wants to show the final enlightenment of Nekhlyudov in *Resurrection* he fails for the same reason that he had failed in trying to affirm the significance of Platon Karatayev for Pierre, or the reality of Levin's spiritual rebirth. What he had not known profoundly himself but had merely aspired to know he could not make convincing in his fictional characters. Tolstoy's religious preoccupations now placed demands on his imagination it could not meet.

He set as epigraph to *The Kreutzer Sonata* Christ's saying that 'there be eunuchs, which have made themselves eunuchs for the kingdom of heaven's sake' (Matthew 19:12). This is the charge that Lawrence brought against Tolstoy, who in his view had 'propagated a great system of recusancy... blaspheming his own strength'. There is no doubt that in the last thirty years Tolstoy would have liked to compel his mind to serve him absolutely, in pursuit of a fixed purpose. Tolstoy becomes unmistakably the exponent of a dogma; literature has to submit to severely utilitarian aims. But though he may have sought to achieve complete abstinence in the flesh, he could not, even for the kingdom of heaven's sake, mutilate his genius. It is an awesome sight, this endeavour of a richly endowed sensuous imagination to renounce all its works and to live according to rule in fasting and self-scrutiny, as an example to errant mankind. Tolstoy in the role of religious thinker has not the extraordinary distinction of Tolstoy the novelist. He is no equal of Pascal, or Jonathan Edwards, or in his own time Kierkegaard. But his moral system acquired immense weight from the sincerity and power of argument with which it was presented. To the social application of this doctrine we must now turn.

7 What then must we do?

In 1881 Tolstoy and his family moved to Moscow for the children's education. Hitherto he had known little of city life in the slums and back streets, and the misery he now came across appalled him. The next year there was to be a census. He seized the opportunity to participate, and called on the two thousand students and others also involved to find out the needs of the poor. The experience with its shock made him write a vivid and impassioned appeal to the public conscience, *What Then Must We Do?* (begun early in 1882 and finished four years later). Tolstoy echoes the question put to John the Baptist when he warned of the wrath to come (Luke 3:10). The dread of a revolution with all its horrors had been troubling his mind, and he gave the same answer as John: 'He that hath two coats, let him impart to him that hath none . . .'. *What Then Must We Do?* is the complement to his *Confession*, and in it Tolstoy shapes a social philosophy which would lay the foundations of a righteous life.

Nothing could be more powerful than the prelude to this doctrine, in the first eleven of the forty sections that comprise *What Then Must We Do?* He tells of his grief and despair when visiting the beggars, prostitutes and layabouts who were so utterly unlike the rural poor. In his own village, he explains, small acts of charity could be effective, and they established good relations between donor and recipient. Whatever disquiet the rich man might feel when contemplating such poverty, at least some measures could be taken, and the problem did not threaten the very basis of the social order. But the hideous things he saw in Moscow sent through him a thrill of passionate rejection such as he had felt thirty years before when witnessing a man guillotined in Paris. Now as then he understood immediately that nothing could justify the abomination. And he soon discovered that palliatives were worse than useless, whether it was the handing over of money or the taking of a destitute boy on to his own kitchen staff. These gestures were embarrassing alike to them and to him – the city poor could not adjust themselves to a lavish giver, the boy soon melted back into the slums.

Tolstoy could find no way to ease his conscience short of acting upon the conclusions forced on him. It now seemed perfectly clear that property was an evil and that money enslaved. This meant he had to abandon his long cherished belief that it was possible to be an enlightened proprietor to the advantage of those who worked for him.

The first Epilogue of *War and Peace* had depicted Nikolay Rostov as the ideal landlord who leaves behind him a good memory in the surrounding villages. His peasants respected him as a real 'master' who put their welfare before his own but would make no allowances for slackness. Nikolay had reckoned with the nature of his work force; and hence the estate prospered. Similarly Levin believed that the landlord who has a proper understanding of his peasants can awaken their interest and so improve production for their good and his own (III xxviii), though this turns out to be very difficult. Tolstoy never minimised the problem of gaining their trust, especially for any scheme that to some degree involved partnership. And yet, as Levin tells the old-fashioned proprietor he had met at Sviyazhsky's, the landed gentry have their 'class instinct' to work each in his own corner and they are inspired 'like the vestals of old, to guard some fire or other'. Levin knows that he 'feels a sort of duty towards the land' (VI xxix).

A countryman for the present uprooted in Moscow, Tolstoy now came to doubt that there ever could be a community of interests between rich and poor. In *What Then Must We Do?* he contrasts not merely the Moscow rich at their ball with the freezing coachman outside. It is the same in the country. At hay-making time, when every man, woman and child among the peasants is out in the fields working almost beyond endurance, from the manor house come the sounds of the piano and of croquet balls. Levin would have been sweating with his peasants; but Levin is no ordinary landowner. Tolstoy now indicts the whole class of proprietors for their wrong way of life, quoting Christ's words that a camel can more easily go through a needle's eye than a rich man enter the kingdom of God.

S. N. Bulgakov comments that where we should expect Tolstoy to propose a plan for ending the wretchedness of the poor, he turns instead to his own guilt. And it is true that, like Christian at the start of *The Pilgrim's Progress*, he thinks primarily of escaping from the city of destruction. The search for righteousness matters to him above all else. Tolstoy frames his question as concerning everybody who has wealth: 'What then must we do?' But the thought that consumes him is agonisingly personal: 'What must I do to be saved?' It would seem to be in the spirit of the Sermon on the Mount, from which there may be extracted a social doctrine of far-reaching consequence, but which deals in the first place with entering the kingdom of heaven.

Tolstoy retreated to Yasnaya Polyana. There he reflected on his experience and came to 'a simple and natural conclusion'. This he expressed in one of his usual homely images: a man who feels sorry for the horse he has ridden too hard should get off its back and use his own legs. The programme that follows is designed to make possible the innocence of a life divested of property. It amazed Tolstoy that the solution was so easy. Each man must take the responsibility for his own needs – his samovar, stove, water and clothes. Thus the new Robinson Crusoe would start afresh on his moral island where others in time could join him. Every day Tolstoy used to go out from his Moscow house to fetch water. He taught himself the cobbler's trade. Manual labour was a necessary part of the blameless life.

While engaged upon *What Then Must We Do?* Tolstoy heard about the ploughman T. M. Bondarev, who had evolved a doctrine of 'bread-labour' in harmony with these conclusions. He interpreted God's command to the fallen Adam, 'In the sweat of thy face shalt thou eat bread', as indicating the basis of a just economic system. Tolstoy wrote a preface for Bondarev's book summarising its message:

Of all the definite duties of man, Bondarev considers that the chief, primary and most immutable for every man, is to earn his bread with his own hands – understanding by 'bread-labour' all heavy rough work necessary to save man from death by hunger and cold, and by 'bread', food, drink, clothes, shelter and fuel ... (M 2, 165)

'Bread-labour', then, as Tolstoy wrote to Bondarev, 'is the first law, and the second, to ensure that the first should be kept, is "Resist not evil".'

On his refusal to meet violence with violence is founded the whole of Tolstoy's social philosophy. It seemed to him that all the institutions of society – its government, law-courts, church, schools and centres of scientific research – were accessaries to the main evil, the tyranny of force exerted by the rich over the poor. In his later writings, and notably in *Resurrection*, Tolstoy ripped off masks to the delight of the radicals, however little they may have cared for his religious and moral system. Maude observes that anarchism such as Tolstoy's or that of Prince Peter Kropotkin, the leader and theorist of the political movement, is bound to be immoderate. 'On the question of Government', he says, 'it is almost too much to expect a Russian to speak with moderation' (G 161). As a publicist Tolstoy had never been cautious, and his moral indignation, for which he could show ample cause, now carried him very far. It has to be remembered that the peasants, whose point of view was so decisive for Tolstoy, had regarded the State, particularly since Peter the Great set vigorously to work on his policy of westernisation, as an alien power and (in Peter's hands) the engine of Anti-Christ. Tolstoy, like the sectarians, would concede nothing to Caesar. This made for difficulties. He and his wife found themselves in stubborn disagreement about what to do with his estate. Money he did not want to touch – yet how, in trying to help the victims of the Samara famine in 1892, could he avoid collecting it for their relief? He became an ardent advocate of the contemporary American economist and reformer Henry George's Single Tax on land, which Nekhlyudov in *Resurrection* expounds to his peasants (ii ix): 'he had a head on him, that Zhorzha', says one. But again, when pressed on this by Aylmer Maude, he was forced to admit that the system required a government to administer it, and ideally he stood against all governments. The need to be consistent caused him much anxiety.

However, the Sermon on the Mount is nothing but a series of hard choices, and its recommendations are drastic.

Before long his teaching began to attract disciples. At the turn of the century many experiments in communal farming were made by Tolstoyans. 'Why do "Tolstoy colonies" always fail?' asked Maude, who had seen the process for himself. About the fact of general failure there can be little question that he is right. As he points out, where there are none of the constraints imposed by property, it is extremely hard to arrive at a common understanding. Once the members of a colony had freed themselves from the influence of money, and escaped the coercion of the State, in theory there should be no problems at all except for those the farmer can never escape – bad weather, diseases of crops or livestock, and stony soil. But the stoniest soil of all proved to be the human heart, and there was no way of abolishing violence altogether.

It is instructive to read the account of the colony at Purleigh by M. J. de K. Holman in *New Essays on Tolstoy* (Cambridge, 1978). A colony could not grow beyond its capacity to support those who worked on the land. What then was to be done with further applicants to join? To exclude them was an act of violence. Labour too for the individual and the commune alike demands discipline. Not all Tolstoyans were disciplined in themselves, and to discipline them as members of the work force would require coercion. And finally, there was the same limitation on the colonies as on a monastery. Tolstoyans could run their farm only by withdrawal from the world. This was easier in liberal England and America in those days than anywhere at the present time; but rates and taxes had still to be paid, and produce sold in the market to support the community. A 'Tolstoy colony' existed so that its members could escape from the taint of a world dominated by property. It suffered – but more extremely, since everything was in the open – from the same contradictions that made Tolstoy's life at Yasnaya Polyana so grievous.

He became a powerful voice for the opposition – towards the end of his life the most powerful in the land. He never shrank from protesting at the misdeeds of government. After the 1905 revolution had failed, a strong leader, P. A. Stolypin, held office as premier for five years until he was assassinated. When repression under him was at its most savage, in 1908, Tolstoy wrote a denunciation of capital punishment which rang round the world, *I Cannot Be Silent*. He addressed the Tsar himself as a fellow human being who needed sympathy and advice, as in his letter to Alexander III imploring him to spare the lives of his father's assassins (L 341). Nicholas II he addressed in the *Appeal to the Tsar and his Chief Ministers* of 1901, published in London, which set out the 'modest and easily realisable desires' of the Russian people. Tolstoy was following in the steps of Alexander Herzen, the great opponent of serfdom in its final years before the Emancipation of 1861; but whereas Herzen had published his views from exile in England, Tolstoy was no less outspoken inside Russia. The government did not dare to touch him, though it harassed his near associates.

Yet the comparison with Herzen should not mislead. Tolstoy knew and admired him, but dissented from his opinions. Herzen was a socialist, who believed therefore in the exercise of State control for the benefit of everyone, whereas Tolstoy looked on the whole structure of modern society as a tower of Babel. He could not accept the division of labour, which only, he thought, became a just expedient when decided upon 'by conscience and reason'. The Marxists saw in the division of labour a process that had gradually alienated the worker from his natural self, making him the appendage to a machine. They intended however not to abolish the system but to organise it according to the workers' needs. Tolstoy was bitterly hostile to specialisation in any form. He could not endure to see women forced to roll cigarettes all day with the feverish intensity of St. Vitus's dance. He attacked all the specialists who contributed to the exploitation of others – the lawyers, the social scientists, even the doctors. His hatred of the existing order, shared by the socialists, went far beyond theirs in the fanaticism with which he wanted to abolish the greater part of contemporary culture. It is only among anarchists like Bakunin, or in Futurist poets like Mayakovsky at the start of his career, that such a will for wholesale destruction of existing forms is to be found. Tolstoy sweeps away most of the heritage which Lenin was not prepared to forgo (just as he would not join Plekhanov in belittling Tolstoy's own work). In *What Then Must We Do?* Tolstoy with indiscriminate gusto fells the philosophers who had been influential in his time. Hegel, Malthus, Comte and Spencer were equally deluded and equally insignificant. Like slashing nettles, it is in a way exhilarating. But only a very confident and superficial judge could maintain, as he does, that Hegel and Malthus are dead letters.

The leaders of the political opposition in Tolstoy's later years, whether Populist or Marxist, found it no easier to come to terms with his very mixed achievement than had Chernyshevsky and the men of the sixties. N. K. Mikhaylovsky, the most influential spokesman of the Populists, was hostile to Tolstoy's religious philosophy, and tried to distinguish between the effects of his 'right and left hands', as explaining the lapses from writing of extraordinary power into passages or even entire works laboured, tedious and hobbled by conscience. Plekhanov was anxious to discourage those who looked for common ground between Tolstoy and Marx. He insisted brutally that Tolstoy had never been more than a 'repentant nobleman', that he could never free himself from class prejudice, and that nobody was farther than Tolstoy from the true socialist. They were two ends of a ring that could not be joined.

Lenin greatly admired Tolstoy as a novelist, recognising the sheer mass and variety of his achievement, and rejoicing, in a conversation with Gorky, that no writer in Europe could equal him. Like the left as a whole he thought Tolstoy second to none in the arts of exposure, and credited him with the highest degree of 'sober realism' when describing the wrongs of bourgeois society. At the same time he deplored Tolstoy's proclivity to play the holy fool, his piety, the vegetarianism he had practised since the early 1880s, and his belief in not resisting evil. The contradictions of Tolstoy, Lenin concluded, were those of peasant Russia as manifested in the upheavals of 1905. Tolstoy, who had adopted the point of view of the 'naïve, patriarchal peasant', he saw as a perfect mirror of the Russian revolution. Lenin wrote his articles in a polemical exchange with Plekhanov. The aim was to rehabilitate Tolstoy in the eyes of dogmatic Marxists who overstressed his class origins. There is no reason to be surprised at the contempt which Lenin shows for Tolstoy's ideological weaknesses, as they clearly seemed to a militant at a time when revolutionary zeal was ebbing and some party members were starting to think that socialism might be combined with God-seeking. For Lenin as for the German revolutionary Rosa Luxemburg Tolstoy was a Utopian socialist looking towards the irrecoverable past. Such notions of felicity in a world protected from the industrial future Tolstoy shared with many among the peasants. In Lenin he collides with the ultimate in westernising thought, and the battle with Chernyshevsky is resumed at a more critical stage.

At this period Tolstoy's main struggle, as always, was with himself in the pursuit of righteousness. He identified with the patriarchal peasant in assuming the only natural way of life to be the agrarian. Rousseau's idyllic notion of rustic simplicity never lost its appeal for him. In *Anna Karenina* Levin, on his way to the conversations about agricultural management at Sviyazhsky's, makes a halt at the house of a well-to-do peasant. It is unusually neat and inviting, and displays the old Russian hospitality with an orderliness not typical of Russia. The old man works his own farm with help from the family and two hired labourers. Everything he sees there deeply impresses Levin, who meditates on this exemplary household while continuing his journey (III xxv).

The features of this establishment are similar to what Wordsworth admired in the Cumberland 'statesmen' or freeholders, who gained their living almost entirely by the family's joint efforts. Wordsworth found in their mode of life a moral worth which the city could not foster. He and Tolstoy are agreed that labour on the land, in primitive conditions that do not however stupefy the intelligence, but give a better insight into the nature of man than the educated are likely to achieve, is the one source of genuine happiness on earth.

It is true that Tolstoy's vision through Levin of this ideal household was recorded some years before he wrote *What Then Must We Do?* However, he still appears to have cherished that image, even though he had become more aware of rural poverty and the inevitable hardships of village life. His recommendations in *What Then Must We Do?* and the subsequent teaching on similar lines are for the most part Utopian, and they make scant allowance for the difficulties that arise in applying them. As a social critic, with his almost uncanny awareness of every situation – nowhere better demonstrated than in the opening chapters of *What Then Must We Do?* – Tolstoy must rate extraordinarily high. As a moral judge of erring mankind he stands in a great tradition, from the Hebrew prophets to his own day. His actual prescriptions for social reform scarcely command the same respect. However, in a century overflowing with ill-conceived schemes for the regeneration of mankind, Tolstoy rose above the vast majority of social reformers because of his emphasis on individual responsibility. He was an impatient man, but impatient because he could not endure to see the sufferings of humanity. Tolstoy asked too much of the race; but his most inexorable demands were put on himself.

8 The significance of art

In 1898 after meditating on the subject for fifteen years Tolstoy published the treatise *What is Art?* Like his notorious essay *On Shakespeare and the Drama*, written in 1903, it has shocked readers by its savage iconoclasm. But while the assault on Shakespeare must be judged an aberration, a headlong argument from false premisses, *What is Art?* cannot be dismissed so lightly. Shaw at least found it very effective in displaying 'so utter a contempt for the objections which the routine critic is sure to allege' (G 105) and considered it 'beyond all comparison the best treatise on art that has been done by a literary man . . . in these times'. Tolstoy cared intensely about art. He had stated in *What Then Must We Do?* that like science it was a necessity for mankind, in the same way as food, drink and clothing. What grieved him was that the art which routine critics approved, and following them the world of fashion, failed to answer the purpose of genuine art as he conceived it.

Tolstoy as always toiled for his conclusions, with the customary grim delight in calling for sacrifice which he was the first to make. But though he threw away much that had been universally valued, the outcome is quite unlike that of his work on *The Kreutzer Sonata*. A forbidding book in some respects, *What is Art?* aims to reform, not to eradicate. It examines the foundations of art in order to build more securely.

He began by reading up from reliable accounts what the aestheticians and philosophers had to say. As so often in his exploration of a subject he found nearly all the authorities unhelpful to him. Early in the treatise he makes his own survey of their views in brisk summary form. But first, preferring as always to work out from personal experience, he describes how once he saw an opera in rehearsal. Tolstoy detested the conventions of opera, and later in the treatise he ridicules the Second Day of Wagner's *Ring*, just as in the Shakespeare essay he would ridicule *King Lear*, with an extraordinarily cold and literal eye which makes him totally unreceptive. Once again it is Natasha's view from the opera-box (II v 9), only with a social indignation she had not felt. At the very outset, on going through the wings, Tolstoy came across a desperately tired stage-hand, like every one else sorely vexed by the whole business. The rehearsal exposed for Tolstoy the enormity of bourgeois art, which had to be supported by many thousands of downtrodden workers. Further on he remarks that the publication of Decadent poetry, unintelligible to the masses, required from them an effort only comparable with that of building the pyramids.

The high culture of Europe rested indisputably for Tolstoy on hideous exploitation and gave nothing to the exploited. Nor even did it mean much to those who proclaimed their enjoyment of its works. Modern art, and particularly that which had developed in the last few decades, he dismissed as a sham, kept going by the idle rich in place of religion. It was frivolous and depraved; those who made it the centre of their lives were deceiving themselves about its importance; and worst of all such art constituted a betrayal.

He believed the function of art is to communicate feeling. It does so by exerting an infectious power which makes available to others in all times and places the very experience of the artist. The feelings that good art thus safely conveys ought to be pure and simple, as they are in Homer, one of his touchstones for truth in art, and should reflect a religious awareness. Until the Renaissance, of which the worldly Boccaccio was the forerunner, art had united people in Christian truth. (He could not, however, accept the reputation of Dante, no less suspect to him than Shakespeare's.) But then the upper classes became godless, and art turned to the purveying of sensual gratification. Being obscure and pretentious it could no longer appeal to the masses. As he listened to Wagner's opera Tolstoy had asked himself what it could possibly mean to 'a respected, wise, educated country labourer' – the final judge of art, as of conduct.

Feeling in Tolstoy's view comes over unchanged by the process of art. He would not have agreed with T. S. Eliot that it is the poet's business 'to express feelings which are not in actual emotions at all'. Art should be utterly transparent, a medium which may perhaps clarify the feeling but does not transmute it, or exploit it for aesthetic ends. Plekhanov pointed out that Tolstoy made similar demands on art to those of Chernyshevsky in his notorious dissertation, *The Aesthetic Relations of Art to Reality* (1855). They might differ about the meaning of life, but their test for reality was the same. It was revealed to the sound sense of working people, and had nothing to do with the illusions of an effete upper class.

It was by music that Tolstoy found himself most easily moved. He had a passionate love for it, and once told his son Sergey that were civilisation to collapse he would regret nothing but the loss of music. Sometimes, according to Sergey, 'music agitated him against his will, even tormented him and he would say: *Que me veut cette musique?*' *Childhood* and *The Kreutzer Sonata* alike testify to its power. The jealous husband in the latter work insists that the Chinese were right to make music a concern of the State, since unmonitored its effects can be so terrible. Beethoven's sonata for piano and violin overpowers his mind, disturbing it to no purpose, and making him feel what he does not 'really' feel.

The Kreutzer Sonata puts in an extreme form Tolstoy's anxiety about the power of art to agitate when it should edify. He feared the indeterminacy of music, which can arouse dangerously vague feeling. The listener finds himself the willing captive of the composer who manipulates his emotions at will. But Tolstoy demanded that art should be responsible. He was suspicious of poetry because the exigencies of metre and rhyme could falsify the feeling they were meant to communicate. Here it was not so much the reader as, in the first place, the writer who became a captive.

However, the songs of the peasants fortified rather than imperilled the moral sense. Sergey Tolstoy comments that his father grew up in the country at a time when song was to be heard everywhere. It accompanied all the activities of peasant life and flourished remarkably. *What is Art?* makes another crucial point from Tolstoy's own experience. He describes how one day his spirits had been lifted by hearing a large choir of

peasant women as they greeted his newly married daughter with
a song of welcome. The performance of a Beethoven piano
sonata that evening showed very badly in contrast. Tolstoy had
no patience with Beethoven's later music – 'artistic ravings'
which he put down to deafness. It was the critics in conspiracy
who had fooled the public into admiring them. Beethoven's im-
itators – he named Wagner, Brahms and Richard Strauss – had
gone still more disastrously astray from 'genuine' music which
like folk-song should be 'simple, clear and powerful'.

Poetry was in no better case than music. At this time there
had begun to establish itself in Russia the 'Decadent' school,
originating in France with Baudelaire and Verlaine, both of
whom he rejected as needlessly obscure, and corrupt in their
moral tendency. But hostile though he was to the Decadents, he
did share their liking for two poets claimed by them as precursors in forming the new sensibility, Fyodor Tyutchev (1803–73)
and Afanasy Fet (1820–92). Both appealed to Tolstoy's sense of
human impermanence in a world of unheeding beauty. Particularly in the 1870s Tolstoy had been delighted with the evocation
of mood and natural scene in Fet's verse, which catches the
most elusive of sentiments on the wing. Eykhenbaum points out
an affinity with it in the episode when Levin, after sleeping on a
haystack, notes a shell-like formation of cloud which, once he
has seen Kitty pass in the summer dawn, dissolves like his over-
night resolutions (III xii).

He also confessed to a 'weakness' for Pushkin's poetry. One
lyric in particular, 'Remembrance', on the theme of hopeless
contrition, never failed to move him. And he was ready to
admit that *Eugene Onegin*, *The Gypsies* and the prose tales,
though varying in quality, were 'all true art'. Nevertheless he
had in the end to castigate Pushkin. A 'man of the people', once
again to be the arbiter, simply would not understand the raising
of a monument to him, hearing of Pushkin's lax morals, his
death in a duel, and the verses he had written about love, 'often
very indecent'. As early as 1862, we may recall, Tolstoy had
declared that only persons of vitiated taste could care for Beethoven and Pushkin.

He demands that art should recover its primal simplicity,

much as the Puritans had called for a return to the austerities of
the early Church. Tolstoy wishes to undo the Renaissance
(which had bypassed Russia) and to recover a truly religious art
in which the whole people could participate, an art that would
express good feeling as the basis of right conduct. Such a view
of art is totalitarian in its demands; and sure enough Tolstoy
goes on to provide an index of forbidden works, and a brief list
of what may be recommended. There are startling casualties –
not only Aristophanes, but the Greek tragedians; not only the
morally reprehensible Shakespeare, but also the conscious
teachers of virtue Dante and Milton (both of whom he confessed to having 'read with great difficulty'); not only 'disgusting'
modern painters of the nude, but also Raphael; most of Bach
apart from his arias – and so on, in what can only be called a
pogrom.

The case is violently overstated, with an exasperation by no
means uncommon in the later polemical writings. His alterna-
tive list of works that may justly be admired does not inspire
full confidence. Nobody will dispute the merits of folk tale and
folk music; nor does it follow that art approved by Tolstoy for
its ideological soundness will necessarily be limited in appeal.
He thought very highly of Millet's drawing 'The Man with the
Hoe', which had set out successfully to 'represent the hard-
working peasant with respect and love'. This is true, but does
not wholly account for its excellence. The highest category for
Tolstoy is Christian art; and below that comes 'good universal
art', lodged in the scheme of salvation rather like the virtuous
pagans in medieval thought. This lower category includes *Don
Quixote*, Molière's comedies (Molière being 'perhaps the most
universal, and therefore the most excellent, artist of modern
times'), *David Copperfield* and *The Pickwick Papers*, stories by
Gogol and Pushkin, and some by Maupassant, whom Tolstoy
regarded as a writer of intermittently strict conscience. Few
would challenge these examples; but those of the highest art,
'flowing from love of God', appear generally to have earned
their promotion because they express humanitarian feelings. In
this category are placed *The Robbers* by Schiller; Victor Hugo's
Les Pauvres Gens and *Les Misérables*; *A Tale of Two Cities*,

A Christmas Carol, The Chimes and other stories by Dickens; *Uncle Tom's Cabin*; Dostoyevsky's novels, especially *Notes from the House of the Dead* (Tolstoy tried reading *The Brothers Karamazov* but gave up); and George Eliot's *Adam Bede*. He once observed that the finest thing in all English literature was the chapter in *David Copperfield* telling of Ham's noble self-sacrifice in the attempt to save Steerforth from the wreck. It is a powerful chapter, in which the storm becomes an overwhelming reality. Yet one has to conclude that its didactic purity was what counted most for Tolstoy, and led him perhaps to write something similar in *Master and Man*.

This criterion is clearly in evidence when he discusses painting, which he understood solely in terms of tableaux and illustrations. A picture had to express a moral fable like the Victorian painting he admired because of its charitable subject – a woman and her daughter are feeding a beggar boy. If the artist failed to achieve the right moral relationship to his work, mastery of technique was in vain. Thus Repin's famous picture of a religious procession in the country, though he did not deny it was highly accomplished, had no meaning for Tolstoy because the artist had taken a neutral stance. On the other hand, Leonid Pasternak's perceptive illustrations of Tolstoy's own novels, particularly *Resurrection*, delighted him. Here the artist combined excellent drawing with a profound sympathy for the author's moral purpose.

Where a story is lacking, Tolstoy judges like the most arrant philistine. He quotes with approval a letter from his daughter Tatyana (who had herself some skill as a painter) deploring an exhibition in Paris of the Symbolists and Impressionists: 'One of them, whose name I could not make out – it was something like Redon – had painted a blue face in profile . . . Pissarro has a water-colour all done in dots . . .'. She had 'looked at the pictures conscientiously and carefully', but all she felt was 'stupefaction and ultimate indignation'.

Thus Tolstoy stands like a dragon across the road of modern art. You pass him at your peril. He may seem to anticipate the crass judgement of Socialist Realism, but it is Tolstoy who speaks, and being such a superb artist himself he cannot be ignored. His ideal of a genuinely popular art, at once profound and simple, may rest on an illusion. It is much easier to understand this view in a country where, as in Tolstoy's day, the oral tradition was yet living. Perhaps it should have been expected of a nineteenth-century novelist whose own work commanded a very large public – though not so large as Dickens's in the Anglo-Saxon countries, where literacy was very much more widespread than in Russia. Artists of every age have longed to achieve work that is both lasting and universal. That indeed was Tolstoy's own triumph; but even in Russia where conditions were more favourable, from the absence as yet of mass journalism, Tolstoy is the last writer to have achieved an enormous success which owed nothing to the adventitious or opportunistic. This cannot be said, for example, of Maxim Gorky, whose fame was partly the result of promotion and political accident. Tolstoy wanted and earned the classical status that comes from telling clearly the eternal verities.

In 1872, before starting *Anna Karenina*, he had told Strakhov: 'I have changed my writing methods and my language'. His standard was to be the language used by the people, which he valued above everything as a 'poetic regulator': 'If you try to say anything superfluous, bombastic or morbid, the language won't permit it . . .' (L 244). The first example of such deliberate simplicity was *A Captive in the Caucasus*, published in that year. *What is Art?* mentions it as one of the two works by Tolstoy himself which his depravity of taste had not ruined. It found a way into his second category, of 'good universal art'; another tale, *God Sees the Truth but Waits*, from the same year, he placed in the higher category of Christian art. It was to be followed by many religious tales in the 1880s. Among the best known of these are *What Men Live By* (1881), *Where Love is, God is* (1885), and *How Much Land Does a Man Need?* (1886). In *What is Art?* Tolstoy cites as a paragon from 'universal art' the story of Joseph. Its author

did not need to describe in detail, as would be done nowadays, the blood-stained coat of Joseph, the dwelling and dress of Jacob, the pose and attire of Potiphar's wife, and how adjusting the bracelet on her left arm she said, 'Come to me', and so on, because the content of feeling in this novel is so strong that all details except the most essential – such as that Joseph went out into another room to weep – are superfluous and would only hinder the transmission of emotion. And therefore this novel is accessible to all men, touches people of all nations and classes young and old, and has lasted to our times and will yet last for thousands of years to come. But strip the best novels of our time of their details and what will remain? (A 244–5)

He goes on to remark that the 'realism' so much admired then would be more fittingly described as 'provincialism'.

Tolstoy's own stories of this period are all written with that degree of conciseness illustrated by Joseph's story. He drew upon many sources in legend and folk tale, and not only from Russian oral tradition, being particularly attracted by the Lives of the Saints as a model to imitate. His stories, in parable form, were designed for the simple reader and were extremely effective, like *The Tale of Ivan the Fool* (1886), recognised by the censorship as a dangerous attack on the existing order. Mikhaylovsky thought they often appealed to the worst prejudices and superstitions of the peasant. He cited *The Candle* (1886) with its appalling punishment of the harsh bailiff, and objected to the fantasy and moral distortion. But Mikhaylovsky admits that Tolstoy never looks down upon his audience, though he too readily fits in with their false conceptions. His authorial voice really does seem to emerge from the hut. He has found the true language of the people, and it can be moulded to assume the dignity of the Old Testament. The outlook in the tales is deliberately archaic, and this naturally displeased a progressive such as Mikhaylovsky. Yet the best of them are undeniably natural classics.

The American novelist W. D. Howells said of Tolstoy that 'he replaced the artistic conscience by the human conscience'. Howells, a sympathiser with his social doctrine, conceded that in Tolstoy's ethics he had often felt 'a hardness, almost an arrogance (the word says too much)', adding 'but in his aesthetics I have never felt this' (G 102). There was 'a vital warmth' in his art because Tolstoy refused to separate it from questions of living.

It would not be easy to argue that Tolstoy's treatise is entirely free from arrogance. Too many acknowledged masterpieces are shoved out of the way by this master himself, who lacked the patience or humility to learn the conventions ruling the art of Aeschylus or of Dante in *The Divine Comedy*. But if what Howells says about the novels is true – that there you find 'the most faithful picture of life set in the light of . . . human conscience' – then Tolstoy's demand for sincerity and the enthusiasm that unites people in mutual understanding has behind it the highest warrant – that of his own work.

Tolstoy once declared, when discussing the requirements of a popular journal, that first of all came intelligibility. 'It is impossible', he maintained, 'to write anything bad in completely simple and intelligible language' (L 276). The mere use of such language does not in itself ensure that whatever is so expressed will be worth hearing, or free from harmful intention. But Tolstoy, like all artists, wrote this prescription for himself. He believed that difficult thoughts must be made plain, and that originality needs no bravura to set it off.

His attitude towards art is deeply responsible, even reverent. He wrote to Strakhov in 1877 that whereas in life lying was 'nasty', it could not destroy life, 'but in art, lying destroys the whole chain which links phenomena, and everything crumbles to dust' (L 303). There have been many reputations in his day and since which before long crumbled to dust because of falsity in the work which contemporaries failed to recognise. Tolstoy's insistence upon truthfulness makes his treatise relevant at all times. Many of the judgements on individual works will have to be discounted; but his emphatic assertion that art is one of the most important activities in human life has been borne out by the success with which in his own country it has fought for the individual conscience.

9 Flight from Yasnaya Polyana

In the middle of one night at the end of October 1910 Tolstoy made a sudden decision to leave home. On 7 November he died in the stationmaster's house at Astapovo, within fifty miles of Yasnaya Polyana.

This sensational event came as no surprise to his intimates. Ever since 1884 when he first set off on an abortive attempt to gain his freedom Tolstoy had contemplated the step, and more than once wrote what was intended to be a valedictory letter to his wife. The immediate causes were domestic, arising from the desperate conflict in which this increasingly estranged pair tore their marriage apart. The interests of his wife – to make life tolerable for the children and to save their patrimony – could not be reconciled with those of Tolstoy himself. He wanted to live as an ascetic and to have the family share his principles. From 1883 a brilliant and domineering disciple, V. G. Chertkov, played the part of evil genius, standing at Tolstoy's elbow to prevent the least concession to Sonya, and acting as chief executive of the Tolstoyan movement. Maude says of Chertkov: 'I never knew anyone with such a capacity for enforcing his will on others.'

The personal tragedy would have signified less had Tolstoy remained a private individual. But, as the celebrations of his eightieth birthday in 1908 had made clear, he now belonged to the world. No living writer had fame such as his; to no other sage did pilgrims flock more readily to seek counsel. Tolstoy's domestic life could not be shielded from publicity. He had fled his home to find solitude and peace; but the secret was soon out. The pressmen and film crews arrived for the kill. Tolstoy's death agony at Astapovo focused the attention of millions. No event had been of such world interest since the Dreyfus trial.

The poet V. F. Khodasevich in a characteristically humane and balanced essay of 1935 entitled 'Tolstoy's departure' saw this event as 'important not only for him but also for mankind'.

It seemed to imply far more than the sudden collapse of an old
man's resolve to do his duty by the wife whom it had become a
torment for him to live with, now that he feared she was trying
to destroy his very soul. Chertkov's part in precipitating the
crisis made it certain that the ideological issue would have due
prominence. And indeed, as Khodasevich remarks, 'Nothing
separates people more deeply, more irremediably, than an idea.'
It was known that for the last thirty years Tolstoy had been
trying to put his ideas into practice. The flight from home could
not be isolated from the doctrine.

Tolstoy would have liked to give away all his property, in the
spirit of *What Then Must We Do?* It seemed to him especially
wrong that an author seeking to benefit mankind should earn,
as he had, a fortune from so doing, and he arranged that all his
works written since 1881 with the one exception of *The Death of
Ivan Ilyich* would involve no copyright. Sonya had been able to
prevent him from giving away the copyright of his earlier writings. Although Tolstoy had renounced his estate in favour of
wife and children, he failed to break entirely with his old way of
life, and his disciples were not satisfied. Tolstoy himself had
long been attracted by the Hindu practice according to which a
devout man entering old age relinquishes all worldly concerns
and goes off to meditate.

In *War and Peace* Princess Marya had briefly entertained the
idea of taking to the road with the female pilgrim Fedosyushka
(II iii 26). But duty to her father and to Prince Andrey's son
restrained her. It was the same with Tolstoy. Sonya in her
growing hysteria was a cross laid upon him which he had hoped
to be able to bear until his death. He could not shed his respons-
ibilities to her and to the family; yet he pined for the freedom
of a pilgrim on the road from one monastery to another. Gorky
tells how moved Tolstoy had been to hear about his acquaintance of student days, V. V. Bervi, whose social conscience had
driven him to embrace poverty, wandering the world with a
canvas umbrella and a parcel of rice.

It also mortified Tolstoy that others should be made to suffer
for his beliefs – Chertkov sent into exile, his secretary N. N.
Gusev arrested and similarly punished – while the Government

was unwilling to touch him. The writer V. G. Korolenko on his first visit to Tolstoy in 1886 was told by him: 'How lucky you are: you have suffered for your beliefs. God does not send me this.' Some years later he surprised Gorky by complaining that his own life was altogether too comfortable, adding 'I want to suffer.'

The discomforts of his position were plain to see. Those who venerated him and became his disciples must often have tried Tolstoy's patience, to judge from the dogmatic harshness and exaggeration with which he sometimes answered their questions. The master himself was restless in a way they were not, because, as Bulgakov said, he could never find more than a temporary repose in the doctrine he had preached. Tolstoy continued 'to live to the full extent of his personality and with all its contradictions'.

Thus besides the exasperation that sent him on the road there were more complicated motives, and it was entirely in Tolstoy's character to undertake a new quest. The purpose of that quest was unclear to him. On leaving home he headed for the convent where his sister Marya had long been a nun. He halted on the way at the Optina monastery, which he had visited before. There it seems that he wanted to talk with a well-known spiritual guide, the *starets* or elder, Father Varsonofy, who was later to try unsuccessfully for an interview with the dying Tolstoy at Astapovo. Tolstoy had, of course, been excommunicated from the Orthodox Church, and Khodasevich comments that no conclusions must be drawn from his earlier desire to speak with the elder. He may have been circling round the Church, 'gropingly, at random'; but it was not evident that he wanted to go in. When Tolstoy's funeral took place on a wooded knoll near his house, there were no religious rites. He could only have been received back into the Church if he would renounce his beliefs. In Orthodox eyes Tolstoy died a heretic.

Berdyayev commented that his homeleaving was an act of genius which had agitated the whole world. It signified 'the conclusion of Tolstoy's anarchic revolt': the wanderer had now turned to mysticism and awaited 'a final revolution'. But this would have meant the overthrow of all his rational thinking, that doctrine of personal salvation which he had made so extraordinarily clear and uncomplicated. Berdyayev is probably wrong: it was intolerable vexation rather than a stroke of astonishing insight that led Tolstoy to break with his past. A new phase of experience undoubtedly lay before him; but, as Bulgakov noted, the rupture had not been complete. At the Optina monastery he was dictating some thoughts on the death penalty. It would appear that his mission as teacher was to continue.

When a man has become like Tolstoy legendary in his own lifetime, a step so drastic as the flight from Yasnaya Polyana is bound to be overlaid by the world at large with symbolic meaning. For many people inside Russia and beyond its frontiers he stood as the guardian of human rights, and the proof that moral rebuke could still turn back governments from wrongdoing. His going out to eventual death moved people's imaginations then, and it has not ceased to do so. George Orwell perceived in this 'a sort of phantom reminiscence of Lear'; Boris Pasternak thought it entirely natural that he should find his peace 'as a wanderer, on the road'; and Isaiah Berlin has compared him with the self-blinded Oedipus at Colonus, 'a desperate old man, beyond human aid'.

His departure left an immense void in the moral life of the nation. 'With Tolstoy', the poet Alexander Blok observed, 'there died human tenderness – a wise humanity.' Once he had quitted the scene, a new drama could begin, as the pitiless twentieth century erupted in continuous wars, revolutions and the uprooting of peoples. Gorky once exclaimed: 'I am not an orphan upon earth, so long as this man is there.' It would hardly be an exaggeration to say that in leaving his home Tolstoy had removed one of the last assurances that could sustain Russia on the verge of upheaval. The action did not cancel his achievement, or the sense of his life, as suicide can; but in more than just physical being he was no longer present. A gulf had suddenly opened, and Pushkin's Russia, still while Tolstoy lived a palpable reality, now lay on the other side.

10 Tolstoy in our time

It was Dostoyevsky's spirit that worked most actively upon Russian literature in the troubled opening years of the twentieth century. A generation was seeking a sign; and the prophetic voice that rang in its ears was not Tolstoy's. The conscience of young thinking Russia found itself in the poetry of Blok. His sense of things can be described as Dostoyevskian. Like many others he had gained strength from the spectacle of Tolstoy's devotion to the truth that makes free; but his own nature was more fallible, and desperately aware of contradictions in itself and in the world. Like Dostoyevsky he moved between ecstasy and negation, with a continual restlessness and foreboding; and like Dostoyevsky he longed to see human life ennobled and liberated from evil, which at the same time held for him an unholy fascination. During the revolutionary summer of 1917, Blok noted in his diary that he had a Rasputin within ('Grishka sits in me'). Tolstoy would have scorned Rasputin as the fitting associate of corrupted rulers; Blok feared him as a fifth columnist in the psyche.

Berdyayev wrote of the 'unbridgeable gap' which separates the admirers of Tolstoy and those of Dostoyevsky (G 215). The former, he said, looked upon Dostoyevsky as 'an unchristian, gloomy, disturbing writer who opens the pits of hell'. Those words were published in 1934, when the pits were revealing new profundities; and it is no wonder that Dostoyevsky's vision has seemed entirely appropriate to our time. Lionel Trilling, some twenty years later, wrote:

> Nowadays the sense of evil comes easily to all of us. We all share what Henry James called the 'imagination of disaster' . . . To many of us the world has the look and feel of a Dostoyevsky novel, every moment of it crisis, every detail of it the projection of exacerbated sensibility and blind, wounded will. (G 275)

Hence he concludes it to be not surprising that 'when the spell of Tolstoy is not immediately upon us,' his work may appear 'a sort of idyll of reality'.

Trilling spoke for what was conscious of itself as being the modern sensibility, guilt-ridden (and hence turning for enlightenment to Freud), deeply distressed by a sense of alienation (which Marx had blamed upon the inhumanity of the capitalist system), and haunted by the apparent prevalence of the absurd and the irrational in human affairs. Trilling has elsewhere sketched out the genesis of 'modern' literature, a long line of subversion which begins with Diderot's dialogue, *Le Neveu de Rameau*, admired by Marx and Freud, and leading on to a work of negation so total as virtually to negate all others, Dostoyevsky's *Notes from Underground* (1864). It has been the office of modern literature to record and intensify the anxieties of the age, diagnosing the sickness of those who live in a diseased civilisation.

Trilling's list of authors in this tradition includes Nietzsche, Kafka, Gide, Thomas Mann, and would be easy to extend into the present day. Tolstoy makes a marginal appearance there, with one story, *The Death of Ivan Ilyich*, admitted because 'so ruthlessly and with such dreadful force' it 'destroys the citadel of the commonplace life in which we all believe we can take refuge from ourselves and our fate'. But Tolstoy even in this story, for all its attack on the complacencies of middle-class life, stands apart from the precursors of the modern, simply by his inclusion of the peasant lad Gerasim. This shows that beyond the nihilism there exists a hope, a confidence in right feeling and in the sense of human responsibility. Tolstoy never for a moment enrolled in the army of the underground. He belongs to the moral tradition which in modern eyes may seem part of the 'idyll' that replaces reality.

For Trilling he is the remembrancer of a 'normal actuality' in which it has become increasingly hard to believe. Another American critic of the same time, Philip Rahv, has contrasted him with Kafka, 'an utterly alienated man, without a past and without a future', whereas Tolstoy was secure 'in possession of the world and of his own humanity' (G 236). But Rahv recognises that Tolstoy too 'could not finally escape the blight of alienation. The long spiritual drama of his final years is a witness to this. Rahv notes the determination with which he resisted the breakdown of traditional values. Tolstoy wrote when ethical questions had not yielded place to problems of psychology, and for him a person's character was unitary throughout life. He held that moral choice was possible and necessary; the individual conscience must not seek refuge from itself in accusing forces outside its control – an unfortunate heredity, a crippling environment, the spirit of the age, the imperatives of party or the exigencies of business.

In the Soviet Union Dostoyevsky was soon relegated to the 'underground', where he belonged. Some years before the Revolution Gorky had written that 'Dostoyevsky is a genius, but our evil genius . . .' And he had asked: 'Can a nation exist that is divided into voluptuary anarchists and half-dead fatalists?' The imagination of Dostoyevsky, he maintained, could conceive only two types – Fyodor Karamazov and the perverse activists who like Verkhovensky in *The Possessed* had politicised his creed, on the one hand; on the other (recalling Platon Karatayev) Fyodor's monkish son Alyosha and the 'idiot', Prince Myshkin. This indictment of Dostoyevsky followed the line of a famous essay by Mikhaylovsky, published thirty years earlier, 'A Cruel Talent' (1882); and in Stalin's time there could be no arguing against it. Tolstoy, however, had been made safe for the new mass reader by Lenin's articles. Isaak Babel, already in disfavour, could say in 1937, after reading *Hadji Murat* again: 'Here the electric charge went from the earth, through the hands, straight to the paper, with no insulation at all, quite mercilessly stripping off all outer layers with a sense of truth . . .' (G 203). But for most Soviet readers Lenin's formulations about Tolstoy acted as a dependable lightning conductor.

How it worked can be seen from an incident in Solzhenitsyn's *Cancer Ward* (1963–6). The patients have come across a volume of Tolstoy's religious tales, among which is *What Men Live By*. Ruslanov, the soundly indoctrinated party official, on hearing that 'love' is the answer given, is able to smell out 'a kilometre away' that 'this isn't our morality.' He mistakes the author for

A. N. Tolstoy, three times a Stalin Prize Laureate, whose work is always optimistic and patriotic, and insists he could never have written such a thing. So it was the other Tolstoy? A quick incantation is required: 'mirror of the Russian revolution', 'rice cutlets', grave ideological shortcomings. But Stalin is now dead, and the danger of Tolstoy's moral candour can no longer so easily be deflected.

Solzhenitsyn is as much Tolstoyan in spirit as Blok had been Dostoyevskian — more evidently so indeed, because he seems consciously to have assumed his mantle. The long series of historical episodes beginning with *August 1914* are recognisably Tolstoyan in conception; the immense dossier of *Gulag Archipelago* is an exposure in Tolstoy's style, and would be a sustained act of 'making it strange' were not the incidents in themselves strange almost beyond belief. Solzhenitsyn through trial and suffering has proved himself the heir to Tolstoy, though it must be obvious that in imaginative power he is more limited. It might seem that the prophetic energies of Tolstoy had looked for another vessel, and Solzhenitsyn were cast for the role of 'great writer of the Russian land'. More accurate perhaps would be the statement that his work and the mission he has adopted testify to the continuing power of Tolstoy's example as guardian of the public conscience.

Jawaharlal Nehru remarks of Gandhi, whose respect for Tolstoy has already been mentioned: 'Much that he said we only partially accepted or did not accept at all. But all this was secondary. The essence of his teaching was fearlessness and truth, and action allied to these . . .'. He claims that Gandhi had found 'all-pervading fear' in India, and raised against it his 'quiet and determined voice: Be not afraid.' These words are no less true of Tolstoy's influence, wherever oppression exists. It is not his teaching that need be accepted, as a prescriptive code of behaviour. The contradictions in this caused Tolstoy himself much vexation of spirit, and a passionate concern for right conduct did not always exclude equally passionate prejudice. Not all his conclusions seem practicable in a world that has become at once more ruthless and less accountable than his. Tolstoy's practical teaching is, then, a secondary matter, and it does not

greatly affect his immense moral significance. He has come supremely to represent the virtues Nehru admired in Gandhi,
fearlessness and truth. Boris Pasternak, unhappy with the hol-
low rhetoric of a Soviet Writers' Congress in 1936, made his
appeal for sincerity by invoking Tolstoy's downright frankness
in opposing the sham. For Tolstoy, when truth is at issue, no
other authority can be tolerated.

Chekhov once wrote of his dismay at the prospect of Tolstoy's death, and the void it would create for him personally.
Tolstoy's career, he thought, justified 'all the hopes and ex-
pectations reposed in literature' (G 111). Russians have always
taken literature with a seriousness that it no longer commands
generally in the West. What Chekhov meant was that Tolstoy
(who, he said, 'makes up for all of us') had never allowed his
writing to become a matter of routine, or an art sufficient to
itself; but he had believed passionately that it must answer the
needs of the entire community. He never lost sight of the millions who in his day were beginning to read, and he was not
deaf to their appeal: 'write for us, who hunger for living words.'
To satisfy that hunger he founded in 1885 with Chertkov and
others his own publishing firm called *The Intermediary*, the aim
of which was to make good writing available to the masses at
the cheapest possible price. It was, however, by his own literary
works above all that he sought to promote the love of truth.
Tolstoy more than any contemporary, even Dostoyevsky, fulfilled the role of the writer as it had come to be understood in
Russia. He kept steadily before him the issues of the day; he
had an unsleeping conscience; and he tried to live in the spirit
of his own teaching. There was no separation for him between
the life of imagination and the life of practical activity. Dostoyevsky the novelist is a much more impressive witness to
truth than Dostoyevsky the publicist, and in his dealings with
others he could be petty, dishonourable and malevolent. Tolstoy writes with a subtler and profounder awareness in his
fiction than in his homilies; but he nowhere prevaricates, and
the effort to be sincere gave him no rest. There is only one
Tolstoy, not always equally effective, but never trying for less
than the whole truth as he saw it.

What is popular, in the sense of being approved without further examination, held no interest at all for Tolstoy. His preoccupation was with something quite different, what is common to all who share in the trials of living, or what Rahv calls 'the most ordinary and therefore in their own way also the gravest occasions of life'. It could be said that Tolstoy restores the weight to such occasions. His hold on common experience was so strong that he could achieve simplicity without shallowness. It is not only in stories deliberately taking up the ideas and idiom of the people that Tolstoy shows himself a universal writer. Russian literature has nearly always been able to break through the limitations of class. Erich Auerbach noted this feature of Russian realism in *Mimesis*, concluding that it was 'based on a Christian and traditionally patriarchal concept of the creatural dignity of every human individual regardless of social rank and position . . .'. Tolstoy is intelligible at once to the simplest reader, and not only because he took such immense pains to make himself clear. It is even more a matter of feeling. He has an immediate effect, for he is always what Wordsworth held the poet to be, 'a man speaking to men.'

Tolstoy rejoiced in art because it gives

> the mysterious gladness of a communion which, reaching beyond the grave, unites with all men of the past who have been moved by the same feelings and with all men of the future who will yet be touched by them (A 240).

The idea had been expressed by Wordsworth in rather similar terms; and Joseph Conrad only a few years after Tolstoy, in 1897, was to speak of the 'conviction of solidarity' to which art responds. Conrad the exile felt to an unbearable degree the loneliness of the human condition; and Wordsworth, more confident of his membership in a simple community among the mountains, is yet at his most inspired moments a solitary. He speaks *for* the country people, but scarcely *with* them. Tolstoy, as individual and intransigent as ever man was, though he doubted so many things in his arduous search for meaning in life, felt the 'conviction of solidarity' so strongly that he always spoke to people of every condition. He did not lament the passing of community. For him its existence was never in question. He foresaw the art of the future as becoming not less but more universal, its forms open to every one, its access to the common experience immediate and free.

Such optimism is not peculiar to him among Russian writers. When Tolstoy was still a child Pushkin had affirmed in a famous poem that his art would be known throughout the length and breadth of the Russian empire, and the people's path to this monument would never be grass-grown. The leading Russian poets of this century have all believed that they write for the people as a whole, who have need of them. In a moment of seemingly fatal isolation, when no editor would touch his work, and the regime was poised to destroy him, Mandelstam could yet state as an unshakeable truth that poetry was a necessity for the people, like light, the blue air, bread and pure snow of the mountain.

That term, the people, has been often manipulated in political discourse, and nowhere more harmfully than in Russia. But the value is still there. Its Russian form, *narod*, has a peculiar resonance which cannot be conveyed in English. It implies the warmth of a family, who are children of the same motherland (*rodina*), and the cognate adjective, *rodnoy*, 'very own', expresses a heart-felt intimacy. Russian literature at its finest is conversation within the family, but the family is hospitable to all. The more truly national a writer in this sense, the more acceptable he becomes to the whole world; and that is the case with Tolstoy.

Of most value today, in a time of worn-down distinctions and slack consensus, is Tolstoy's almost pedantic effort to get things straight. He had, as we have seen, an inveterate suspicion of the 'poetic', which in *What is Art?* he states baldly is none other than 'the borrowed'. The nihilist Bazarov in Turgenev's *Fathers and Children* (1862) impatiently tells his friend and admirer, the sentimental Arkady, to cut out the fine talk; and Tolstoy is no less unceremonious. He envied Turgenev at one time for the accomplishment of his style, but came to realise the dangers inherent in grace and euphony when they are made paramount. Gerard Manley Hopkins distinguished between the inspired language of a poet and what he called the same poet's 'Parnassian', by which is meant a characteristic manner that relies on its habitual skill and does not exert itself. Turgenev too often falls into Parnassian; Tolstoy subjected his writing to the same fierce scrutiny that he brought to moral conduct. Few authors have dealt so drastically with their proof-sheets. He returned again and again to the clarification of what he was trying to say. And it is this deliberate avoidance of ornament which gives such confidence in what he tells. Matthew Arnold on reading *Anna Karenina* was struck by what he supposed to be Tolstoy's artlessness: 'The author has not invented and combined it, he has seen it.' This was a naïve comment, though not perhaps surprising when we recall that Arnold read Tolstoy in French, and so was led naturally to compare his novel with Flaubert's *Madame Bovary*. Babel was much better informed on this question than Arnold, but he records a similar impression. 'When you read Tolstoy,' he says, 'you feel that the world is writing.' The effect is like that of Blok's poetry, as described by Pasternak. You open the printed page to find not merely 'verses about the wind and puddles, streetlamps and stars': the puddles have actually been there, and their damp and disturbing traces are left on the paper.

Tolstoy lent his art to no purposes other than the finding and definition of truth. He had desired fame, and he was not free from vanity; but he never wrote to please or to incite admiration. The only good opinion he sought was from his own conscience, which never allowed him to forget the responsibility of the artist. To an astonishing degree he was endowed with the life-giving touch. Even in the latest of his fictions, *Hadji Murat*, there is a host of characters, each living the moments of an unique life. Tolstoy's power of attention is like the sun, illuminating whatever lies in its path, steady and equal. He is creative in the manner of the great Renaissance artists, or of Homer whom he so much desired to emulate. This solidity and range of his talent make him classical. They speak to us of a bygone age, of a plenitude that seems in his pages inexhaustible, but has now vanished.

Taking the measure of his achievement has not been easy.

Because he went to such pains in elaborating a philosophy when he had already written his greatest novels, the ideas he expressed seem to require the same attention as is given to the thought of metaphysicians and theologians. Tolstoy invaded their ground all too confidently, and those who have been trained in these disciplines can point to his false premises and crude simplifications. They may still admire his boldness in cutting through what he held to be sophistry, but cannot overlook that he did so at his own peril.

So it is necessary once more to insist upon Tolstoy's much greater importance as a creative writer. Had he not wanted·to be more than a novelist, to explore and overcome the thought of his age, to legislate for mankind, he could not have achieved what he did in fiction. The Russian novel in his day was a marvellous instrument for the study of human life at the meeting-point of a traditional past and a menacing future. Tolstoy lacked the prophetic insight of Dostoyevsky into that future. His 'naïve reverence for the reasonable', as Berdyayev describes it, would not let him enter that 'new era in the inner history of man' disclosed by Dostoyevsky, Nietzsche and Kierkegaard. But that limitation was also a source of strength. Tolstoy stands for recognition of the continuity in human experience, for the possibilities of renewal, and for the natural energies that will not be baulked.

His finest work shares the peculiarity of all great imaginative writing, that it can be read many times with fresh insight. The connections it reveals are so various that on each return something new comes to the fore, and the ordering is subtly different. He remains one of the most satisfying of the world's writers because he saw so much that the reader takes to be true of human experience in all ages. Our discontents today may appear to us overwhelming and inescapable. But Tolstoy, when his imagination exerts itself fully as it so often does, in the most extraordinary way stabilises the reader's mind, and justifies each individual life in the sense of its own significance.

Bibliographical Note

The best life of Tolstoy is still that by Aylmer Maude, in two volumes (Oxford, 1930). However, Henri Troyat's vivid and detailed *Tolstoy* (trans. Nancy Leroux, London, 1970) was able to draw upon ampler sources.

The translations by Louise and Aylmer Maude in *The Centenary Edition of Tolstoy* in 21 vols. (Oxford, 1928–37) remain supreme, and have been used in this book. Available in The World's Classics paperback editions are *Anna Karenina* and *The Raid and Other Stories* (includes *Albert, What Men Live By*, and *Master and Man*); *War and Peace* is forthcoming. I have discussed the relative merits of the Maudes, Rosemary Edmonds (in the Penguin Classics) and Constance Garnett as translators in *New Essays on Tolstoy*, ed. Malcolm Jones (Cambridge, 1978). This volume makes a useful supplement to *Tolstoy: A Collection of Critical Essays* ed. Ralph E. Matlaw (Englewood Cliffs, New Jersey, 1967).

It is invidious to pick out only a few of the many good books on Tolstoy published in recent decades. But two contrasting studies should certainly be recommended: John Bayley's *Tolstoy and the Novel* (London, 1966) and R. F. Christian's *Tolstoy: A Critical Introduction* (Cambridge, 1969). Isaiah Berlin's celebrated essay *The Hedgehog and the Fox* (London, 1953; reprinted in *Russian Thinkers*, London, 1978) deals with Tolstoy's view of history. *Tolstoy: The Comprehensive Vision* by E. B. Greenwood (London, 1975; reissued 1980) is valuable for its handling of Tolstoy's ideas, and the study by Edward Wasiolek *Tolstoy's Major Fiction* (Chicago and London, 1978) has some penetrating insights. Boris Eykhenbaum's three volumes on Tolstoy are now all available in English: *The Young Tolstoi* (trans. Gary Kern, Ann Arbor, 1972); *Tolstoi in the Sixties* (trans. D. White, Ann Arbor, 1982); *Tolstoi in the Seventies* (trans. A. Kaspin, Ann Arbor, 1982).

A. V. Knowles has edited the Tolstoy volume in the Critical

Heritage series (London, 1978) which contains much criticism by Tolstoy's contemporaries.

R. F. Christian's selection, *Tolstoy's Letters* (London, 1978), is admirably made and has excellent notes. When quoting from the Letters, I append a reference: in each case the whole letter is worth reading.

Index